WORDS OF WISDOM SERIES

The principal objective of THE MATHESON TRUST is to promote the study of comparative religion from the point of view of the underlying harmony of the great religious and philosophical traditions of the world. This objective is being pursued through such means as audio-visual media, the support and sponsorship of lecture series and conferences, the creation of a website, collaboration with film production companies and publishing companies as well as the Trust's own series of publications.

The WORDS OF WISDOM SERIES makes available previously unpublished or rare materials in which the immediacy of the live speech goes hand in hand with the penetration into the hearts of the religious traditions.

ENDURING UTTERANCE

•

COLLECTED LECTURES (1993–2001)

كَلِمَةً طَيِّبَةً كَشَجَرَةٍ طَيِّبَةٍ

A good word is as a good tree

Enduring Utterance

Collected Lectures

(1993–2001)

WORDS OF WISDOM SERIES I

by

Martin Lings

edited and introduced by

Trevor Banyard

THE MATHESON TRUST
For the Study of Comparative Religion

The Matheson Trust
PO Box 336
56 Gloucester Road
London SW7 4UB, UK
www.themathesontrust.org

ISBN: 978 1 908092 09 0

British Library Cataloguing-in-Publication Data.
A catalogue record for this book is available from the British Library.

The publishers wish to thank
The Temenos Academy
for their co-operation in the production of this work.
Audio recordings of most of the talks in this volume are available from them and from the Matheson Trust website.

Typeset by the publishers in Baskerville 10 Pro

Contents

Preface

The chapters of this book are based on transcripts of various talks delivered by Dr. Martin Lings. It was Dr. Lings' custom to prepare notes which he would use as cues for the different points he wished to mention in a talk. This would not be a script from which he would read, but an *aide memoire* that permitted him a degree of spontaneity that gave his talks a certain personal touch whilst keeping within a given topic. It also meant that he might elaborate during the course of a talk on one aspect on a certain occasion more than he might have done at another time, even though the talk as a whole would revolve around the same basic themes.

It is almost inevitable that an edited transcript should differ from the talk itself, as the spoken words of even the most eloquent speaker differ from what he might compose as a text. Therefore, what I have attempted to do here is render the spoken word as a written text with minimal adjustment, which is indeed the editor's job, and is a view that Dr. Lings himself is known to have expressed. I have tried to eliminate any repetition or hesitation which occurs quite naturally in spontaneous speech. I have also tried to retain something of the immediacy and vitality of the spoken word in the various chapters, without transforming them into a dissertation or reducing them to the flatness we might encounter in a scholarly textbook. I take responsibility, and apologize in advance, for any omissions or errors that may have occurred during the compilation.

All manifestation derives from a Primary Cause, apart from

which nothing can exist. Therefore all things are interconnected in one way or another due to their relationship to this Cause, which they share in common and of which they are reflected aspects. Martin Lings dedicated his life to the search for this Principle which expresses itself in many forms.

In these times when religion is subject to criticism from various quarters, it can be helpful to approach the topic from the top down, rather than the other way round. In other words, from the point of view of the Absolute. It is easy to censure religion by highlighting particular shortcomings, limitations and omissions, or by comparing the differing dogmas and concluding that they cannot all be true, or that none of them are true. But we live in a world of contingencies, and it is this world that the religions occupy, being particular irruptions of a common source into a realm of discrete phenomena where we generally fail to perceive the interconnectedness of all things.

Thus, the chapters are arranged in an order that begins, in a sense, with the more universal and leads on to the more specific. Those talks which deal primarily with the major plays of Shakespeare appear in a sister volume.

Trevor Banyard

Metaphysics and the Perennial Philosophy

MY TALK IS CALLED *Metaphysics and the Perennial Philosophy*, the word "metaphysics" coming first; that is not an important detail, but it explains why I begin by mentioning that René Guénon only once, as far as I know, entered into the academic world, which he did in answering an invitation from the Sorbonne University in Paris to give a talk on metaphysics. And in that talk, which was entitled *La Métaphysique Orientale*, he began by saying that it would perhaps be better just to say metaphysics, *la métaphysique*, without any epithet, because pure metaphysics, being beyond all form and all contingencies, is neither Eastern nor Western: it is universal. He meant by beyond "form," of course, beyond any particular religious form, and by "contingency," the demands of perspective and the demands of human capacity. He objected also to the English "s" on the end of "metaphysics"; he said, "Why do you not call it 'metaphysic'? why this plural?" It is not really a plural, of course, it means that it comes "after physics": *meta*-physics.

Now, Guénon would have accepted as a partial synonym for "metaphysical" the word "supernatural," only on condition that "supernatural" is taken to mean "beyond this world" and, microcosmically speaking, "beyond body and soul." Frithjof Schuon sometimes speaks of the metacosm, meaning the next world rather than this world, and the metacosm in this sense is the lowest domain of metaphysics; the highest domain being at the divine level itself, and the summit being the Absolute. Metaphysics comprises all this domain, from the Absolute-Infinite-Perfection of the divine Essence to the lowest of the Paradises of the next world.

To go back to that summit which is sometimes called the divine Essence, tradition is universal in this. In Hinduism, *Brahma*—the neuter form of the word—and also *Atma*, which means Self, denote this Absolute-Infinite-Perfection, and both *Brahma* and *Atma* are expressed by the divine monosyllable *Om*, and they are referred to as *Tat*, which means That.

This oldest living esoterism is identical in its metaphysical doctrine with Sufism, which is the youngest living esoterism. Here, the divine Essence is also absolutely beyond duality, and beyond duality is what the Hindus mean by *Advaita*. Advaita Vedanta is the Hindu equivalent, therefore, of Sufism. And in Christianity, you all know I think, that Meister Eckhart insisted that beyond God in the ordinary sense there is the Godhead, and he insisted on making this distinction, which created a certain scandal in the Vatican.

According to metaphysics, this one metaphysical doctrine, only Absolute-Infinite-Perfection is real; all else is illusion. In Hinduism, the word *Maya* is used for illusion. In Islam—in Sufism, that is—it is called the "veil," *ḥijāb*, and in both traditions, illusion begins already at the divine level, as soon as there is any question of duality, of manifestation or creation. The monotheistic religions speak of creation, but on the inward side, esoterically, Sufism, like Hinduism, speaks of manifestation. Everything that exists is a manifestation of the Absolute-Infinite-Perfection. Creation or manifestation is the first hint of relativity, that is, of illusion, and this begins at the level of the personal God.

For the ancient Greeks—for Plato—this Absolute was *to agathon*, the Good, and Saint Augustine, you will remember, said it is in the nature of the Good to communicate Itself; and there is a saying in Islam, where God speaks on the tongue of the Prophet: *I was a Hidden Treasure and I loved to be known, and so I created the world*—to manifest *My Hidden Treasure*. Here is the beginning of illusion: it is a mystery that the Absolute-Infinite-Perfection remains immutable; It cannot change; It is not affected by Its own manifestation, which is illusion, and which proceeds from Him. Just as it proceeds from Him, it returns to Him. Frithjof Schuon sums this up wonderfully in the words, "Being what It is, the Absolute cannot not be immutable, and It cannot not radiate. Immutability, or fidelity to Itself, and radiation, or gift of Itself. There lies the essence of all that is."[1]

The great Algerian Shaykh Aḥmad al-ʿAlawī, in one of his poems, speaks of illusion, the veil, that is, everything which proceeds from God. He says: "It is Hidden in Its own Outward Manifestation wherein It doth appear as Veil after Veil made to cover Its Glory,"[2] that is, the Truth, the Reality, is hidden in Its own outward manifestation, and It appears in this outward manifestation as veil after veil, made to cover Its Glory.

As I said, the lower boundary of metaphysics can be placed at the lowest of the Paradises, and the barrier between the next world and this is represented in many different ways. Here again, in the different expressions of metaphysics in the different traditions the same symbols are used. For example, in Genesis we have the words: *The Spirit of God breathed on the face of the waters... and the waters were divided.*[3] Hinduism also speaks of the upper waters and the lower waters. The division of the waters is the distinction between this world, the lower waters, and the next world, which is the higher waters, and the boundary between the two is what I am just going to speak about now.

1 Frithjof Schuon, *From the Divine to the Human*, Bloomington IN: World Wisdom Books, 1982, p. 42.

2 The Shaykh al-ʿAlawī, *Dīwān*, in Martin Lings, *A Sufi Saint of the Twentieth Century*, 3rd ed., Cambridge: Islamic Texts Society, 1993, p. 220.

3 Genesis, I: 2 and 6.

In Islam one has also in the Qur'ān mention of the two seas: one salt and bitter (the lower waters, this world), the other fresh and sweet (the next world, the world of the Heavens and the Paradises). And in ancient Greece one has another very striking symbol: the *Symplegades*, the Clashing Rocks. When the Argonauts went in search of the Golden Fleece, the Clashing Rocks were held apart by the goddess Athene to allow them to pass. The Golden Fleece is clearly representative of all that Man had lost at the Fall. The Qur'ān says, *if you would pass beyond the boundary of Heaven and Earth* (and by Heaven here it does not mean the Heaven of the next world, it means simply the sky) *do so, but you cannot pass without authority*.[4] In my book *Symbol and Archetype* the second chapter is called "The Decisive Boundary," and it is about this particular boundary, which is very important, of crucial importance to us all, because it is that beyond which we have to go, and beyond which even lies what is called spiritually "the heart", joined often in the expression the "eye of the heart." That eye is still in the domain of metaphysics, because it is on the other side of the boundary from here. The Golden Fleece was in the domain of metaphysics.

Another symbol is the passage of the Children of Israel across the waters of the Red Sea. That again is an example comparable to the Greek, since God held the waters of the Red Sea apart just as the goddess Athene held the Clashing Rocks apart; and so the Children of Israel were able to pass across, but the sea came together and drowned their enemies. The passage through this Narrow Gate—in the words used by Christ, *Enter ye in at the narrow gate*[5]—is a difficult passage one has to pass through, symbolised in many different ways.

The word "transcendent" strictly speaking coincides with metaphysics. That "trans-" is in the word *meta*, and the word "transcendent" can only be used of what lies beyond the

---

[4] Qur'ān, 55:33. [5] St Matthew, 7:13.

Clashing Rocks, beyond the Narrow Gate, and beyond the barrier—the *barzakh* in Arabic—which separates the two seas.

As to the word "sacred," which sometimes is synonymous with "transcendent" but is more general, this world was in the beginning sacred, but now the word "sacred" can only be applied to what here below is impregnated with spiritual significance, because what is here below has become polluted, corrupted. What is impregnated with spiritual significance are the divine Messengers, the founders of religion, and those saints who prolong and protect their messages throughout the ages, throughout the centuries. Likewise sacred are the works of sacred art, which are crystallisations of sanctity in stone, and their counterparts in poetry and music. But first of all we must include virgin nature itself, which was created to manifest the Absolute-Infinite-Perfection.

Now, metaphysics is included in *sophia perennis*, in perennial philosophy, as that which concerns the intelligence, but man is not only intelligence. Anything that can be called religion, *religio perennis*, must concern not only part of man, but the whole of man, and man is not only intelligence. Nor is his intelligence altogether in the domain of metaphysics.

When I was a student at Oxford, I was privileged to have C. S. Lewis as my tutor, and I remember a lecture he gave on the mediaeval perspective that prevailed in England in the time of the 13th or 14th century, and he mentioned that it was dominated in many respects by what had been written by Boethius; and according to Boethius, the human intelligence has four levels: firstly—I will give the Latin terms as used by him, because they are easy to understand—*intellectus*, then *ratio*, then *imaginatio*, then *sensus*: Intellect, reason, imagination and the senses. Of those four faculties, only one is in the domain of metaphysics, and that is the Intellect. I remember Lewis emphasising that the Intellect, alone of the faculties, is directly concerned with the transcendent, with the beyond, with the Hereafter. Of the other faculties, reason is, or should be, the handmaid to the Intellect. The Intellect itself is only concerned with what lies beyond, what is transcendent, in other words, with metaphysical truth.

Metaphysical doctrine means "teaching." Teaching what? By "what" I mean, "What is it that receives the teaching?" The Intellect? no. I am not using the word "intellect" in the modern misuse of the word, because as you know, it is used to mean simply "intelligence" in modern language, but in the correct sense of the Latin *intellectus* as used by Boethius.[6] Metaphysical doctrine is not addressed to the Intellect, because the Intellect does not need teaching, being itself metaphysical; it has direct perception of metaphysical realities, and in any case, in the vast majority of men today the Intellect is veiled, so that it cannot be reached by teaching in any case. We will come later to what metaphysical teaching is addressed to, but it is not addressed to the Intellect.

The Intellect is universally recognised as being enthroned in the Heart, and what is meant by "heart" in the inner aspect of the different religions is not the centre of the body, but it is the centre of the soul: the Heart as the centre of the psychic substance. And you have all heard mention of the Eye of the Heart, and only that eye can perceive metaphysical truth directly, and that sight is what man lost at the Fall. Hearts became veiled; this is a universal doctrine, and one finds it in all religions. The Qur'ān says: *It is not the eyesights which are blind, it is the hearts in the breasts which are blind.*[7] In the "Beatitudes" we are told: *Blessed are the pure in heart, for they shall see God.*[8] That sight is always associated with the Heart. The Prophet of Islam said: *My heart is awake like the hearts of the prophets before me.* The "wake" of the Heart means that it can see; the eye is open. And the main purpose in all esoterisms is to open that inward eye which is blind in the soul.

Eckhart was referring to this when he said, "There is

[6] Hence the capitalisation of Intellect in this transcription.
[7] Qur'ān, 22:46. [8] St Matthew, 5:8.

something in the soul which is uncreated and uncreatable... and this is the intellect;"[9] and this is the Intellect in the true sense as used by Boethius, and it is the Intellect which sees the metaphysical realities of the next world. That is what the inner aspect of religion is concerned with; wherever one goes, Hinduism, Buddhism and the three monotheistic religions in their mysticisms are all concerned primarily with this.

It is as if at the Fall of Man human consciousness had been abstracted from the Heart, and then drawn out backwards and downwards through the Narrow Gate in the wrong direction, between the Clashing Rocks, again in the wrong direction, so as to be imprisoned altogether in this world. In other words, at the Fall man lost the direct sense of the Transcendent. Hence, the need for metaphysics, which is, as we have seen, the doctrine of the Transcendent.

To go back to the question of teaching, in some very exceptional cases, that doctrine can unveil the Intellect, if it is not too heavily veiled, in a flash of light, as it were, and that is sometimes called "intellection"; but that is a grace which no one has the right to rely on as a possibility for oneself. The main function of metaphysics has to do with what we call intuition. The Heart is, as we have seen, on the other side of the Narrow Gate and the Clashing Rocks, but the human mind is not immediately on this side of that Gate. Above the mind there lies what we sometimes call the higher reaches of human intelligence, and these reaches are the domain of intuition. I will come back in a moment to the effect of metaphysics in this domain, but first of all I must say a word about the perennial philosophy.

There is, at the end of one of Frithjof Schuon's books, the English version of which is called *Light on the Ancient Worlds*:

> It has been said more than once that total Truth is inscribed in an immortal script in the very substance

[9] Meister Eckhart, Sermon 24.

> of our spirit; what the different Revelations do is to "crystallize" and "actualize," in different degrees... a nucleus of certitudes that not only abides forever in the divine Omniscience, but also sleeps by refraction... in the kernel of the individual...[10]

In other words, according to the perennial philosophy, total Truth is inscribed in the depths of every human being, where in most cases today it sleeps "in the kernel of the individual." But it sleeps in different degrees.

There is a reference to *religio perennis* implicitly—not, of course, explicitly—in Sophocles' play *Antigone*; a very moving passage. The situation is as follows: the two sons of Oedipus have been fighting against each other in a civil war and both brothers are killed, and after the battle Creon, the King of Thebes, gives an order that the brother who was loyal to Thebes shall be buried with all honours, but that the other brother, who was fighting against the city, his body must be left on the battlefield to rot, and nobody must bury it. Antigone is their sister, and she goes to the king and says that he cannot make this decree, that he must allow her to bury the brother; even though he was fighting against the city, he must allow her to go out and bury her brother, and he refuses. And she says, *I did not think that you would be capable of acting against the unwritten and unfailing statutes of the gods: these are not of today nor yesterday, but from all time, and no one knoweth when they were first put forth*. That is a very clear reference to *religio perennis*, something which, as Schuon says, is inscribed in our intelligences, and it is something universal. It is not a question of how a body is to be buried, whether to be burnt, or whether to be placed in the earth; it is a question of the fact that the living are under the obligation to look after their dead. They cannot abandon them. This is an aspect, which Antigone understood, of these *unwritten and unfailing statutes of the gods*.

---

[10] Frithjof Schuon, *Light on the Ancient Worlds*, London: Perennial Books, 1965.

And there lies the tragedy: she disobeys Creon and—well, you might look at the play for yourselves, because it is indeed a wonderful play.

I will again quote what Frithjof Schuon says about the development of the cycle:

> In the Golden Age men lived on the memory of the lost Paradise, and on their inward religion that was *religio perennis*. They did not need an outwardly revealed religion. Then men became affected by passions to the point of forgetting certain aspects of Truth, and religions like Hinduism were revealed. But when passions dominated men, still more religions were needed, like the last three of this cycle of time, but each one has an inner aspect like the older religions which is centred on metaphysical truth.[11]

Again, I will quote from Schuon, and this is to do with metaphysics, and it is very relevant to this talk:

> Knowledge saves only on condition that it enlists all that we are. Only when it is a way which tills, and which transforms, and which wounds our nature as the plough wounds the earth. Metaphysical knowledge is sacred; it is the right of sacred things to demand of man all that he is.[12]

What is this "all"? I mentioned earlier, in connection with metaphysics, that man is not only intelligence, and this "all" is intelligence, will and character, or one could say instead of character, soul or psychic substance. And that is why the revealed religions, which deal with man and are for man, are always threefold. There is always a doctrine, there is always a method, and there is always a moral aspect; of these three, doctrine relates to the intelligence; it is the will that has to impose the method; and morals concern the psychic substance—they are the virtues. Every religion is Truth, Way and Virtue.

---

[11] Frithjof Schuon, adapted from *Esoterism as Principle and as Way*.

[12] *Spiritual Perspectives and Human Facts* (Perennial Books, 1970), p. 138.

To go back to the question of metaphysical teaching, I said that it is concerned first of all with the intuition, which lies in what we may call the higher reaches of the psychic substance, beyond the mind, but on this side still of the Narrow Gate and the Clashing Rocks; not yet in contact with the Heart directly, but nonetheless, metaphysical teaching creates in the domain of the intuitions vibrations. When the seeker hears metaphysical truths, vibrations will be made in the higher reaches of his intelligence, and these vibrations should normally awaken corresponding vibrations in the deeper reaches of the will, because, relatively speaking, we can speak of height and depth. The domain of the intuitions is objective in a certain sense; the domain of the will is more subjective; and these vibrations in the deeper reaches of the will are rather subjective vibrations corresponding to the objective vibrations of the intuition. And the will, thanks to these vibrations, chooses the Absolute rather than the relative; it chooses the Infinite rather than the finite; it chooses the Eternal rather than the ephemeral; and the will says to the soul, "I have decided that we shall follow a spiritual path."

But here comes the main problem of a spirituality: the will cannot say to the soul, "and you will like it." In other words, you can lead a horse to the water, but you cannot make it drink. And that is the great problem, because, if the horse does not drink, then everything is lost, or rather, no progress can be made. And here is the origin of what in Islam is called the Greater Holy War. Returning from a victory in one of his last military campaigns, the Prophet said: *We have returned from the lesser holy war to the greater holy war*, and they said to him, *What is the greater holy war?* and he said, *The war against the soul.*[13]

The problem here is that the soul is made up of multiple elements. In fallen man these elements are in chaos, and many of them are dormant, and they all have to be put in their right

[13] A hadith often quoted by the Sufis and reported by Ghazālī in the *Iḥyā' ʿulūm al-dīn*.

place; they all have to be won over, and that is why something like war may be said to take place. The means of war are, as you know, different kinds of asceticism, for example. All that has to do with compelling the soul to submit, because the soul has to come to love spirituality. It is only then that unity can be established in the soul of the seeker, and then there is no longer any difficulty or any problem.

In his book *Echoes of Perennial Wisdom*, Schuon says something very pertinent to this: "It is all very well for the intelligence to affirm metaphysical and eschatological truths"—eschatological has to do with our final ends—"the imagination and the subconscious continue to believe firmly in the world, not in God, not in the Hereafter."[14] And in another passage elsewhere, he says, "The Way calls for a re-education and a regeneration of imagination and feeling, which are falsified by the world."[15] It is in fact the world that determines them, whereas they should live on the concrete consciousness of our final ends. This is the great difficulty which is faced in spirituality, and it explains a lot of what one reads of mystical treatises in the different traditions.

Another quotation, again from Schuon, is a particular truth which I have never come across anywhere but in his writings. I have often quoted it myself:

> The usual religious arguments, through not probing sufficiently to the depth of things, and moreover not having previously had any need to do so, are psychologically somewhat outworn, and fail to satisfy certain requirements of causality. If human societies degenerate, on the one hand, with the passage of time, they accumulate, on the other hand, experiences in virtue of old age, however intermingled with errors these may be. This paradox is something that any pastoral teaching intended to be effective should take account of, not by drawing new directives

[14] World Wisdom, Bloomington, Indiana, 2012, p. 6. [15] *Book of Keys*, 642.

from the general error, but by using arguments of a higher order, intellectual rather than sentimental.[16]

An example of these errors of what pastoral teaching should not do, and which is continually being done, is the argument previously used that there is only one religion. Each religion claimed to be the only one, the only effective religion. That is now outworn, simply because man, the collectivity, has accumulated by old age a certain wisdom, and it will not accept things like that, which were accepted in the Middle Ages. They were true in a sense, because if a person is practising one religion, practising it well, faithfully, in a concentrated manner, it is for him the only religion. In that particular sense, there is a saying by a Sufi shaykh that if a person wants to find water, he will dig in one place; he will not start digging in one place and then go somewhere else. In that way he will never find water, but if he continues to dig in one place he will in the end find water. But today such an argument works in a different manner; it is a good argument, it has not lost its goodness, but it does not work as regards there being only one religion, because people are now in contact with many other religions, and they see there must be more than one true religion, and God cannot have deceived most of humanity.

As for "drawing... directives from the general error." That is significant, because the other day only, the Pope announced that he saw nothing in the teachings of Teilhard de Chardin contrary to religion. It is ironical, because the Church latterly has always been a little behind the times, and now, when more and more scientific books are being written and published proving scientifically that the doctrine of evolution is false, and that all scientific evidence is more on the side of Genesis than on the side of Darwin, the Vatican, in order to be up to date, has to come in at this late hour and say a good word for

16 *Form and Substance in the Religions*, ch. 16, "The Human Margin".

Teilhard de Chardin. That is an example of drawing directives from error, the existing error.

Schuon goes on to say, speaking of basic human values, where does a man's spiritual worth lie? Is it in his intelligence? his discernment? his metaphysical knowledge? Obviously not, if this knowledge is not combined with a realising will, and with an inclusive virtue, or virtues which are at least sufficient. Is it his realising will which constitutes his worth? his power of concentration? No, if this is not combined with the necessary minimum of doctrinal knowledge and with virtue. And spiritual worth likewise does not consist in virtue, if this is not accompanied by a doctrinal understanding that is at least sufficient, and by an equivalent realising effort.

Obviously the most brilliant intellectual knowledge is fruitless in the absence of the corresponding realising initiative, and in the absence of the necessary virtue. In other words, knowledge is nothing if it is combined with spiritual laziness and with pretension, egoism, hypocrisy. Likewise, the most prestigious power of concentration is nothing if it is accompanied by doctrinal ignorance and moral insufficiency. Likewise again, natural virtue is but little without the doctrinal Truth and spiritual practice, which operate it with a view to God, and which thus restore to it the whole point of its being.

And Schuon says as regards the spiritual effort: "Remove the rust from the Heart, and the Intellect will be released." That is, as I said, the essential concern of all spirituality, especially at the beginning. The Eye of the Heart is veiled, and in Islam, in Sufism for example, they speak of rust over the Heart, hence "remove the rust from the Heart." That means that the Eye will be able to see, and the Intellect will be released. He goes on to say, "This release is strictly impossible—we must insist upon it—without the co-operation of a religion, an orthodoxy, a traditional esoterism, with all that this implies."

Let me end my talk with just mentioning that the existence

of such writings as these places a very great responsibility upon us. We are all, whatever our years, old, because of what I have just recently quoted. We are living at the end of the cycle. One might ask: "Well, what is the difference between us and the Middle Ages? Five hundred years, what is five hundred years in a cycle which consists of many thousands of years?" But the answer is that in the Middle Ages, that old age of the cycle was overlaid by the youth of Christianity and the youth of Islam. Now, both Christianity and Islam are clearly in their old age, so that there is no youth to rejuvenate this old age, and that is why everybody today is old; whether they are young in years or old in years, they all have a certain old age, and with everybody the question arises: "Which aspect of old age are we to choose? the positive aspect or the negative aspect?" The fact is that the vast majority of people, without realising it, have chosen the negative aspect, which is senility. We have the possibility of choosing the positive aspect of old age, which is wisdom. Each one of us—theoretically speaking, at any rate—has that possibility. So let us reflect on this, and let us make our choice.

René Guénon

THIS IS A VERY LARGE SUBJECT I have undertaken, and I am going to do what I can; but as regards the life of René Guénon—the early part of his life, at any rate—our knowledge is very limited because of his extreme reticence. There must have seldom been a man so objective as he was, and his objective view of the world, which is one aspect of his greatness, made him realise the evils of subjectivism and individualism in the modern world, and he seems to have applied this to himself even, rigorously—almost too rigorously. He shrank, in any event, from speaking about himself. After his death, book after book has been written about him, and the authors have no doubt felt often extremely frustrated, being unable to find out various things, and book after book contains factual errors, often small details, but nonetheless the books are full of mistakes.

What we do know is that he was born at Blois, in France, in 1886, that he was the son of an architect, he had a traditional Catholic upbringing, and at school he excelled in philosophy and mathematics. But at the age of twenty-one he was already in Paris in the world of occultism, which was in full ferment at that time, just after the turn of the century, about 1907, and the dangers of that world were perhaps counteracted for him by the fact that it was more open to wider perspectives. And it seems to be about this time that he came in contact with some Hindus in Paris, some Hindus of the Advaita Vedanta school, and one of them initiated him into their own Shivaite line of spirituality. We have no details of time or place, and he does not ever seem to have spoken about these Hindus, and after one or two years he does not seem to have had any more contact with them. But what he learned from them is in his books, and his meeting with them was clearly providential. His contact with them must have been extremely intense while it lasted, and his books are just what was, and is, needed as antidote to the crisis of the modern world—that is the title of one of his books, *The Crisis of the Modern World*[1]—and the perspective of his books largely coincides with the Hindu perspective. But by the time he was thirty—probably before then—his phenomenal intelligence had enabled him to see exactly what was wrong with the modern Western world, and that same intelligence had dug him out of it altogether.

Now, I remember that world. At least, I remember practically nothing before the First World War. But I do remember the world into which, and for which, Guénon wrote his first books, and that was in the first decade after the war. That monstrous world was made impenetrable, as has been said, by euphoria. But the First World War did not make any difference to that really, because that was the war to end war. After the First World War the euphoria was even worse. Now there would never be another war, and science had "proved" that man was descended from the ape, that is, he had progressed from the ape, and this progress would continue now with nothing to impede it. Everything would get better and better and better.

I remember I was at school at that time, and I remember being taught these things, with just one hour a week being taught the opposite by a religious lesson; but religion in the modern world had long before then been pushed into a corner. From its corner it protested against this euphoria, but to absolutely no avail.

Today the situation is considerably worse and considerably better. It is worse because human beings have degenerated

---

[1] First published as *La Crise du monde moderne*, Paris: Bossard, 1927.

still further; one sees far more bad faces about than one did in the twenties, if I may say so. That is my impression; it may not be everybody's impression. It is better because there is no euphoria at all. The edifice of the modern world is falling into ruin; great cracks are appearing everywhere through which it can be penetrated as it could not before. But it is again worse because the Church, anxious not to be behind the times, has become the accomplice of modernity.

But to return to the world of the twenties, I remember a politician proclaiming, as who would dare to do so now: "We are now in the glorious morning of the world." And at this same time, Guénon wrote of this "wonderful" world: "It is as if an organism with its head cut off were to go on living a life which was both intense and disordered." That is fairly strong. That is from his book *East and West*,[2] which was published in 1924.

As I said, Guénon seems to have had no further contact with the Hindus, and no doubt they had returned to India. Meantime Guénon had been initiated into a Sufi order which was to be his spiritual home for the rest of his life. But among the ills he saw on every side about him, he was very much preoccupied with the general anti-religious prejudice that was particularly rife among the French so-called *intelligentsia*, and he was sure that some of these people were nonetheless virtually intelligent and would be capable of responding to the Truth if it were clearly set before them.

It is not difficult to see why there was this anti-religious prejudice, because the representatives of religion were less and less intelligent, more centred on sentimental considerations; and in the Catholic church, especially where the division of the community into clergy and laity was always stressed, a lay figure had to rely on the Church, for it was not his business to think about spiritual things, and he had to rely on the clergy. Intelligent laymen would ask questions of priests who would

2 *Orient et Occident*, Paris: Payot, 1924.

be unable to answer them, and who would take refuge in the idea that intelligence and pride were very closely connected. And so it is not difficult to see how this very anti-religious prejudice came into being, especially in France.

Guénon put himself the question: "Since these people had rejected Christianity, would they be able to accept the Truth when expressed in the Islamic terms of Sufism?"—which were closely related to Christian terms in many respects. He decided that they would not, that they would say: "But this is just another religion, and we have had enough of religion." But Hinduism, the oldest living religion, is, on the surface and in its manner of speaking, very different from both Christianity and Islam, and he decided to confront the Western world with the Truth on the basis of Hinduism. And to this end he wrote his *General Introduction to the Study of Hindu Doctrines*.[3] This is one of the books that was translated and published by Marco Pallis and Richard Nicholson. The French was published in 1921, to be followed in 1925 by what is perhaps one of the greatest of all Guénon's books: *Man and his Becoming According to the Vedanta*.[4]

He could not have chosen a better setting for his message of Truth to the West, because of Hinduism's directness, which results from its having been revealed to man in a remote age when there was not yet a need to make a distinction between esoterism and exoterism. That directness means that the Truth did not have to be veiled. Already in classical antiquity, the Mysteries, that is, esoterism, were for the few, but in Hinduism they were the norm, and the highest truths could be spoken out directly. There was no question of *Cast not your pearls before swine* and *Give not holy things to dogs*.[5] Also we must remember that the caste system in India, which has been the object of untold attacks, was precisely the preserver of Hinduism. It

[3] *Introduction générale à l'étude des doctrines hindoues*, 1921.

[4] *L'homme et son devenir selon le Vedântâ,* Paris: Brossard, 1925.

[5] St Matthew, 7:6.

is thanks to the caste system that Hinduism has remained more or less intact down to the present day, whereas its sister religions, for example, the religions of Greece and Rome, have long since perished. The caste system with the Brahmins as safeguarders of religion is responsible for the fact that we have today a Hinduism which has not decayed and is still living, and which down to this century has produced flowers of sanctity.

One of the points to be mentioned first is the question of the distinction which has to be made at the divine level, and which is made in all esoterisms, but which cannot be made in exoterism, in religion as given to the masses today: the distinction between the Absolute and the beginnings of relativity. The Absolute, which is One, Infinite, Eternal, Immutable, undetermined, unconditioned, is termed *Atma*, which means Self, and *Brahma*,[6] which is a neuter word that serves to emphasise that it is beyond all duality, such as male and female. It is also termed That, quite simply, *Tat*, just as in Sufism the Absolute is sometimes termed "He," *Huwa*. The Absolute is represented in Hinduism by the sacred monosyllable *Om*.

Then we have what corresponds in other religions to the personal God, *Ishvara*, which is the beginning already of relativity, because It is concerned with manifestation—the term the Hindus use for Creation—and Creation is clearly the beginning of a duality: Creator and created. *Ishvara* is at the divine level, but It is the beginning of relativity, and in all esoterism one has this same doctrine. It may be recalled that Meister Eckhart came into difficulties with the Church because he insisted on making a distinction between God and Godhead, *Gott* and *Gottheit*, and he used the second term for the Absolute, that is, the absolute Absolute, and *Gott* for the relative Absolute. It could have been the other way round, but

[6] The neuter *Brahma* (as opposed to the masculine) is equivalent to *Brahman* (see below).

it was just that he needed to make some difference. In Sufism one speaks of the divine Essence and the essential Names of God, such as "The One," "The Truth," "The All-Holy," "The Living," and one or two other Names like that. "The Infinitely Good" also, and by that I mean *al-Raḥmān*, which contains the roots of all goodness, but which is a Name also of the divine Essence. And below that there are the Names which are called the Names of Qualities, like Creator, for example, and "The Merciful," in the sense of "One who has Mercy," and so on, and that is clearly the beginning of a duality. In every esoterism one has this distinction made even at the level of the Divinity. One cannot have it below esoterism because it would result in the idea of two gods, and a division in the Divinity would be exceedingly dangerous in the hands of the mass of believers. It would cause all sorts of problems, and the Divine Unity has to be maintained at all costs.

Guénon in this book traces with wonderful clarity the hierarchy of the Universe from the Absolute, and from the personal God, down to the created *Logos*, *Buddhi*, which also means Intellect, and which has three aspects which are named *Brahma*—but this time the word is masculine—*Vishnu* and *Shiva*. In the hierarchy of the Universe these three aspects are called *Deva*, which is the word for god, the same word linguistically as the Latin *Deus*, but strictly speaking they have the rank really of what we would call Archangels. They are created, but Hinduism is so subtle that they can be invoked, because they descend from the Absolute and they return to the Absolute. They are symbols of the Absolute, and they can be invoked in the sense of the absolute *Brahman*, of *Atma* and of *Om*. That is why one has in Hinduism the invocations of *Brahma*, *Vishnu* and *Shiva*.

The Hindu doctrine, like Genesis, speaks of the two waters. The Qur'ān is the same; it speaks of the two seas, which are the Upper Waters and the Lower Waters. The Upper Waters represent the higher aspect of the created world, that is, the manifested world, corresponding to the different Heavens in which are the different Paradises. It is all part of the next world from the point of view of this world. The Lower Waters represent the world of body and soul. And all is a manifestation of the Absolute. Having traced the manifestation of Man and shown what is the nature of Man in all its details, Guénon then proceeds to show how, according to Hindu doctrine, Man can return to his absolute source.

This book[7] is a really remarkable doctrine in itself. It ends with the supreme spiritual possibility of oneness with the Absolute, a oneness which is already there, and, as may well be known, a Brahmin boy at the age of eight, when he is initiated by his father, the words are spoken into his ear: *Thou art That*, meaning: "Thou art the Absolute," *Tat tvam asi*. This shows how far we are from the outer aspect of religion in the modern world. But that truth which is called in Sufism "the Secret," *al-Sirr*, is present necessarily in all esoterism in the present day, otherwise it would not deserve the name of esoterism.

Another aspect of Hinduism which made it a perfect vehicle for Guénon's message is the breadth of its structure, considering the doctrine of the *samsara*, that is, the chain of endless worlds which have been manifested, of which the Universe consists. In the later religions it is as if Providence had shepherded mankind into a narrower and narrower valley. This is providential in that the opening is still the same, always to Heaven, but the outlook on the sides, the horizontal outlook, is narrower and narrower, because man is no longer capable of taking in more than a certain amount; to have the vast aspect which the doctrine of the *samsara* gives us would lead to all kinds of distractions. But nonetheless, when one is speaking of an Absolute, Infinite, Eternal Divinity, the idea that that infinitude produced only one single world in manifesting Itself does not satisfy the intelligence. The

[7] *Man and His Becoming According to the Vedanta.*

doctrine of the *samsara* does, on the other hand, satisfy, in that the worlds are innumerable that have been manifested.

Another point is that Hinduism has an amazing versatility. First of all, it depends on divine Revelation; it makes an implacable distinction between Revelation and inspiration. The Vedas are revealed, the *Upanishads* are revealed, the *Bhagavad Gita* is generally considered as revealed, directly revealed in the sense that the Pentateuch was revealed to Moses and that the Qur'ān was revealed to the Prophet. But this distinction between Revelation, *Sruti*, and inspiration, which is *Smriti*, is made very clearly in Hinduism, and that is something which, of course, Christianity does not have, and the Christians as a rule do not understand that distinction. They have difficulty in realising the distinction of the Pentateuch, that is, Genesis and the other books in the Old Testament, for example, and the Book of Kings and Chronicles, which are simply sacred history: inspired perhaps, but in no sense revealed. The Psalms, on the other hand, are also revealed.

Hinduism also has the *Avatara*s, and that a Christian can well understand, that is, the manifestations, the descents, of the Divinity. Of course, a modern Christian would not recognise the descents of the Hindu *Avatara*s, because for the average Christian there has only ever been one descent, and that is Christ Himself. But Hinduism recognises that as a possibility, and it has ten *Avatara*s who have helped maintain the vitality of the religion down to the present day. And the ninth *Avatara*, which is called the foreign *Avatara*, is the Buddha himself, who, although he appeared in India, was not for Hindus, but clearly for the part of the world east of India.

The breadth of Hinduism is also seen in its prefiguration of exoterism, which is a recognition of the three ways, the three *marga*s. These three ways back to God are the way of knowledge, the way of love and the way of action, three ways which correspond to the inclinations and affinities of different human beings.

Another point which makes Hinduism so right for Europeans, that is, to give them the message in those terms, is that they have as Aryans an affinity with Hinduism, because they are rooted in the religions of classical antiquity. These are sister religions to Hinduism, and their structure was clearly the same as the structure of Hinduism, but, of course, they degenerated into complete decadence and now have disappeared. Nonetheless, our heritage lies in them, and so Guénon gives us, one might say, the possibility of a mysterious renaissance, in a purely positive sense, by his message of the Truth in Hindu terms. But this affinity must not be exaggerated, and Guénon never in fact advised anybody, as far as I know, to become a Hindu. He advised Hindus to remain Hindus, but he never advised anybody who was not a Hindu to become a Hindu.

His message was always one of strict orthodoxy in one esoterism, but, at the same time, equal recognition of all other orthodoxies. Yet his purpose was in no sense academic. His motto was *vincit omnia veritas*, "Truth conquers all," but implicitly this was *Seek and ye shall find; knock and it shall be opened unto you*,[8] and implicit in his writings is the certainty that they will come providentially to those who are qualified to receive his message, and that this would impel them to seek and therefore to find a way.

Guénon was conscious of having a function, and he knew what belonged to this function and what did not belong to it. He knew that it was not his function to have disciples, and he never accepted any. It was his function to teach in preparation for a way that people would find for themselves, and this preparation meant filling in gaps—many of the tremendous gaps—which are left by modern education.

[8] St Matthew, 7:7.

The first of these gaps is failure to understand the meaning of the transcendent, and the meaning of the word "intellect" in consequence, a word which always continues to be used. The word "intellectual" is a favourite word on people's lips, but the Intellect in the true sense of the word, in the traditional sense, corresponding to the Sanskrit *Buddhi*, had simply been forgotten in the Western world. Guénon insisted in his writings on giving this word its true meaning, which is perception of transcendent realities, the faculty which can perceive the things of the next world. Its prolongations in the soul are what might be called intellectual intuitions, which is the preliminary glimmering before intellection in the full sense takes place. One has the impression—but this is pure assumption on my part—that Guénon himself must have had a remarkable intellectual revelation at quite an early age, that he must have perceived directly spiritual truths with the Intellect in the true sense.

He also fills in gaps by explaining the meaning of rites, the meaning of symbols and the hierarchy of the worlds, because in modern education the next world is left out altogether, whereas, in the Middle Ages, students were taught about the hierarchy of the faculties, and correspondingly, the hierarchy of the Universe.

I must for the moment speak on a rather personal level, but perhaps it may not be without interest. When I read the books of Guénon—in the early thirties it must have been—it was as if I had been struck by lightning. I realised that this was the Truth, and that I had never seen the Truth before set down. This message of Guénon that there was not only one religion and all other religions false, that there were many religions and they must all be treated with reverence. They were all on a level, but they were different because they were for different people. It made sense, and it also was at the same time to the glory of God, because a person with even a reasonable intelligence, when taught what we were taught at school, would inevitably think: "Well, what about the rest of the world? why were things managed in this way? why was the Truth given first of all to the Jews, one people only, to such a small group of people? And then Christianity was ordered to spread over the world, but why so late? why not before? what about previous ages?" and so on. These questions were never answered, but when I read Guénon I knew that this was the Truth, and I knew that I must do something about it, and I wrote to Guénon. I translated one of his first books, *East and West*, into English, and I was in correspondence with him in connection with that. In 1930, after the death of his first wife, Guénon left Paris and went to Cairo for twenty years. He died at the beginning of 1951.

When I read Guénon's books my first idea was to send them to my greatest friend, who had been a student with me at Oxford, because I knew that he would have just the same reaction as I had, which he did in fact. He came back to the West and, like myself, he sought and found a way of the kind Guénon speaks of in his books. He was in need of work, and he was then given a lectureship at Cairo University, and having got there he managed to discover Guénon's address. Guénon was extraordinarily secretive; he would not give his address to anybody. He wanted to disappear. He had enemies in France, and he suspected that they wished to attack him by magic. I do not know this for certain, but I know that Guénon was very much afraid of being attacked by certain people, and he wished to remain unknown, to sink himself into the Egyptian world, the world of Islam.

My friend had great difficulty in finding where he was, and still more difficulty when he did write to him finally to ask if he could see him. It took a very long time for that to take place, but finally Guénon agreed to see my friend. This friend of mine was a very intelligent and very charming person, and Guénon became immediately attached to him, and he told him that he could always come to his house whenever he liked.

In the summer of 1939 I went to visit my friend in Cairo,

and when I was there the war broke out. I was lecturing in Lithuania at that time, which was an independent country, but I was unable to get back. I was forced to stay in Egypt, and my friend took me to see Guénon. My friend at that time was doing everything; he was just like a member of the household. He went and collected Guénon's letters from the poste restante; he did all sorts of things for him. A year later, I was out riding in the desert with my friend when his horse ran away with him, and he was killed as the result of an accident. He died of loss of blood. And I shall never forget having to go to tell Guénon of his death. When I did, he just wept for an hour.

The result of that was that I had to take my friend's place. I also was given the freedom of the household, and very quickly I became like one of the family. It was a tremendous privilege, of course. Guénon's wife could not read and she could only speak Arabic. I quickly learnt Arabic, so I was able to talk to her. It was a very happy marriage, and unexpectedly they began to have children. They had been married for seven years without any children, and Guénon had no children by his first wife, and he was getting fairly old. He was much older than she was, but finally they had four children altogether.

I went to see Guénon sometimes almost every day, and I was the first person to read *The Reign of Quantity*[9]—the only book he wrote while I knew him, because the other books were all written before that time—which he gave me chapter by chapter; and I was able to give him also my own first book when I wrote it, *The Book of Certainty*,[10] which I gave him also chapter by chapter. It was a very great privilege to have known such a person.

During this time a rather important question was resolved. The Hindus with whom Guénon had made contact in Paris

[9] *Le Règne de La Quantité et les Signes des Temps*, Editions Gallimard, 1945.
[10] Abū Bakr Sirāj al-Dīn, *The Book of Certainty*, Cambridge: Islamic Texts Society, 1992.

had given him a wrong idea; they had given him not a strictly Hindu idea about Buddhism. Hinduism recognises the Buddha as the ninth *Avatara* of Vishnu, but some Hindus maintain that he was not an *Avatara*, he was just a revolted *Kshatriya*, that is, a revolted member of the royal caste against the Brahmins. Guénon had accepted this idea, and he wrote about Buddhism as though it was not one of the great religions of the world. Coomaraswamy, Frithjof Schuon and Marco Pallis all together decided that they would remonstrate with Guénon about this point, and Guénon was very open to being persuaded. I think it was in 1946 when I took Marco Pallis to see Guénon, and the result was that he agreed that he had been mistaken, and that things must be changed in his books that he had written about Buddhism. Marco Pallis started sending him a list of all sorts of pages and other things that needed correction. That was a very important point.

Guénon never went out practically, and I only went out once with him. He did come out to visit us; I would send a car to fetch him, and he would come with his family to our house about twice a year. We lived at that time just near the pyramids outside Cairo. But I did go with him once to visit the mosque of Sayyidnā Ḥusayn in the centre of Cairo, near the Azhar. He had a remarkable presence, and it was very striking to see the respect with which he was treated. As he entered the mosque one could hear people on all sides saying: *Allahumma ṣalli ʿalā Sayyidinā Muḥammad*, that is, "May God rain blessings on the Prophet Muḥammad," which is a way of expressing great reverence for anybody. He had a really luminous presence, and his very beautiful eyes were one of his most striking features, and they retained their lustre into early old age, because he did not live to be more than sixty-four. I think he was sixty-four when he died.

With his book on the Vedanta ranks his book on symbols, which was published after his death from all the articles that were written about symbols in his journal, which was the Paris journal, *Études traditionnelles.* It was marvellous to read these articles when they came out, I remember, month after month. Those of you who do not read French and who are able to read it in English I am sure will be fascinated by it. It takes us back almost to prehistoric times, as does *Man and His Becoming According to the Vedanta*, but in a wider sense. *Fundamental Symbols* is the title of the book, and the subtitle is *The Universal Language of Sacred Science.*[11]

Everything is a symbol, of course, everything that exists—it could not exist if it were not a symbol—but the fundamental symbols are those which express eloquently aspects of the supreme Truth and the supreme Way. For example, one of these aspects of both the Way and the Truth is what is called the Axis of the World, the Axis which runs through all the higher states from the centre of this state. That is the meaning of what is called the Tree of Life, which, as is known, is symbolised by many particular trees: the oak and the ash, and the fig, and other trees throughout the world. And the Axis is the Way itself, the Way of return to the Absolute. It is also symbolised by man-made things: the ladder, the mast, weapons like the lance, the central pillar of edifices; and as architects know, many buildings are built round a central axis which is not in fact there, which is not materialised. Very often in traditional houses the hearth was the centre of the house, and the smoke rose up through the chimney, which was also another figure of the axis. And things which are normally horizontal: a bridge is also a symbol of the Axis of the World. Witness the title *pontifex*, the "maker of the bridge," which

[11] First published in French as *Symboles fondamentaux de la Science sacrée*, Gallimard, 1962. Second, revised edition published in French as *Symboles de la Science sacrée*, Gallimard, 1977. English translation of the first French edition published as *Fundamental Symbols: The Universal Language of Sacred Science*, tr. Alvin Moore, Jnr, Quinta Essentia, Cambridge, UK, 1995. English translation of second French edition published as *Symbols of Sacred Science*, tr. Henry D. Fohr, Sophia Perennis, 2004.

is given to the highest spiritual authority, who is the bridge between Heaven and Earth.

In this book on symbols another fundamental symbol is the river. There are three aspects to the river, for example, the crossing of the river symbolises always the passage from this world to a higher world. But then there is the river itself. There is the difficulty of moving upstream, which symbolises the difficulties of the spiritual path, returning to one's Source against the current. But there is also the symbolism of moving in the other direction, to the ocean, returning finally to the ocean. That is also another symbol of the Way.

In this book also Guénon treats of the symbolism of the mountain, the cave, the temporal cycle. In the temporal cycle the solstices of summer and winter are the gates of the gods and ancestors according to Hinduism; the gate of the gods is the winter solstice in the sign of Capricorn, and the gate of the ancestors is the summer solstice in the sign of Cancer.

As I said, Guénon did not like to talk about himself, and I respected his reticence. I did not ask him questions, and I think he was pleased with that. But just to sum up what his function was, one might say that it was his function in a world increasingly rife with heresy and pseudo-religion to remind twentieth century man of the need for orthodoxy, which itself presupposes firstly a divine intervention, Revelation, and secondly a tradition that hands down with fidelity, from generation to generation, what Heaven has revealed.

In this connection we are deeply indebted to him for having restored to the world the word "orthodoxy" in the full rigour of its original meaning, that is, "rectitude of opinion," a rectitude which compels the intelligent man not merely to reject heresy, but also to recognise the validity of all those faiths that conform to those criteria on which his own faith depends for its orthodoxy. On the basis of this universality, which is often known as *religio perennis*, it was also Guénon's function to remind us that the great religions of the world are not only the means of man's salvation, but that they offer him beyond that, even in this life, two esoteric possibilities which correspond to what were known in Graeco-Roman antiquity as *mysteria parva* and *mysteria magna*, the Lesser Mysteries and the Greater Mysteries. The first of these is the way of return to the primordial perfection which was lost at the Fall; the second, which presupposes the first, is the way to gnosis, the fulfilment of the precept *gnothi seauton*, "Know Thyself." And this one ultimate end is termed in Christianity *deificatio*, "deification"; in Hinduism *yoga*, "union," and *moksha*, "deliverance"; in Buddhism *nirvana*, that is, extinction of all that is illusory; and in Islamic mysticism, that is, Sufism, *taḥaqquq*, which means "realisation," which was glossed by a Sufi shaykh as "self-realisation in God."

The Mysteries, and especially the Greater Mysteries, are explicitly or implicitly the main theme of Guénon's writing. Even in *The Crisis of the Modern World* and *The Reign of Quantity*, the troubles in question are shown to have sprung ultimately from the loss of the mysterial dimension, that is, the dimension of the Mysteries, of esoterism. He traces all the troubles in the world to the forgetting of the higher aspects of religion.

He was conscious of being a pioneer, and I will end simply by quoting something he wrote of himself: "All that we shall do or say will amount to giving those who come afterwards facilities which we ourselves were not given. Here, as everywhere else, it is the beginning of the work that is hardest." Well that is, I think, all I can say.

Frithjof Schuon and René Guénon

LADIES AND GENTLEMEN, our friend there who introduced me[1] put an idea into my head, but it is to do with René Guénon. My talk is entitled "Frithjof Schuon and René Guénon," because I propose mostly to speak about the first one, having already given a talk on René Guénon alone. And it was rather strange that the town of Blois in France, where Guénon was born, decided eventually—because he has been very famous in France for many years—they decided to name a street after him; and somebody sent me a photograph of the sign of this street, which said: "Rue René Guénon, philosophe orientaliste."

Well, Guénon was always precisely attacking the philosophers and the orientalists; he refused to be called by either of those names. But it would have been very difficult to find any other words, in fact, which would have been comprehensible to the Frenchmen of Blois that described him so well as that. One could have said "sage"; that is the best description for both these men about whom I am speaking, that they are sages, quite simply,[2] but the word "sage" is no longer used, and it sounds rather vague to a modern European.

Well, to begin my talk: esoterism is the main theme of both these writers. Even their criticisms of the modern world are centred on the almost total absence of any esoterism powerful enough to counteract modernism in the modern world. One might ask the question, "What do you mean by esoterism?"

1 This talk was introduced by Shusha Guppy.

2 Shusha Guppy mentioned the word "sage" in her introduction.

It could be described as the inner aspect of religion, which is summed up by the words of Christ, *The Kingdom of Heaven is within you,*[3] and also the words, *Seek, and ye shall find; knock, and it shall be opened unto you.*[4] That is what is meant by esoterism: the inner aspect of religion, that is, the inner aspect which gives a direct way to God.

But both these writers inevitably wrote about exoterism also, because each religion is one whole, and there is no esoterism apart from orthodox religion. Also, esoterism itself consists always—it is in the nature of things—of circles within circles within circles; *Many are called, but few are chosen.*[5] And they wrote about the religions in general, especially Frithjof Schuon, who said to me once: "If there were a religion which I did not love, I would not rest until I loved it," and by "religion" he meant also what surrounds every great religion. One has only to use the phrase "the great religions of the world," and everybody knows what is meant, because they are unmistakable, and they have certain aspects always. Each of the great religions of the world has a civilisation attached to it, with all the sciences and arts that one expects. It has, going back to the beginning, saints in every generation—at least one or two in every generation, and all these things are part of what Frithjof Schuon loved, when he said that "If there were a religion which I did not love, I would not rest until I loved it."

Both writers were in agreement about essentials, but they were very different in their manner of writing. Guénon, of course, was the great pioneer that had to lay the foundations. He died at the very beginning of 1951, and Schuon's first great book was only published in 1948, so one of them, as it were, possesses one half of the century, the other the second half. It no doubt suited Guénon's function as a pioneer that as a writer he could be likened to an archer; his teachings are like

[3] St Luke, 17:21. [4] St Matthew, 7:7; St Luke, 11:9.
[5] St Matthew, 20:16 and 22:14.

arrows, arrow after arrow, shot from a basis of undeliberating certitude. Most of the arrows hit the centre of the target, and this gives a certain spontaneity of writing which is undeniably attractive. I was privileged to be the first reader of one of his greatest books, *The Reign of Quantity and the Signs of the Times*,[6] and he gave it me chapter by chapter as he was writing it. He never had his books typed, but he sent them in manuscript to the publisher.

But this was during the war, and I insisted on having the book typed before it was posted, because I thought it may never reach its destination and might be lost. So when he gave me the last chapter, he said: "Now I will make a fair copy of the book," and then he gave me the fair copy to have it typed. But there was no difference between the fair copy and the rough copy. He wrote straight as the thoughts came to him, and he did not correct anything. There it was written and there it stayed. Whereas the rough copies of Schuon's writings are pieces of paper with things pasted over them, all sorts of crossings out and rewritings. Most of the typescripts of Schuon's books had to be retyped more than once, because of all the changes made. He thought over everything very carefully and weighed everything up; he was his own severest critic. Yet some of Guénon's arrows did go a little wide of the mark. It is a pity, and I think something must be done, if there is time, to salvage them. One or two of the books are really not publishable, because they have certain mistakes, but they have wonderful passages, and it would be a pity that they should not be salvaged, perhaps by way of an anthology of extracts.

Yet Schuon was a providential complement to Guénon, because he never simplifies anything. When he is attacking something, he goes as far as is legitimately possible to meet the person he is attacking on their own ground, if he is attacking the holders of an opinion against which he is arguing. In other words, his theses are worked out in detail, with all

[6] *Le règne de la quantité et les signes des temps*, Gallimard, 1945.

possible objections foreseen, met half way, given their due, and outweighed by what he says.

By way of an example, let me mention his first main book, which I have just referred to, which was published in 1948, *The Transcendent Unity of Religions*. It was just two years before Guénon's death, and this is the only book of Schuon that Guénon ever read, in fact. He had read some of his articles. Schuon had published in 1935 a small collection of profound and very poetical meditations, but they were published in German, which meant that they were less widely distributed than they would have been if they had been in French. Schuon was bilingual, and all his other books are written in French. But in *The Transcendent Unity of Religions* there arises the question of missionaries, in particular Christian missionaries, since the book is written primarily for the modern West; and one can see that the title of the book, *The Transcendent Unity of Religions*, rather precludes the idea of a missionary, but nonetheless, Schuon does justice to the missionaries first of all. He points out that the life of a missionary is a life of great sacrifice, and he admits that in some cases it has even subjectively a mystical value, because it is a very hard life. And he allows that there are relatively rare cases where an individual is more suited to a religion other than that of the world where he was born and brought up. But he reminds us also, and I quote his words: "It is possible to pass from one religious form to another without being converted, which may happen for reasons of esoteric and therefore spiritual expediency." He is referring there to something which, of course, has nothing to do with missionaries. He says "without being converted," and he gives no example, and he passes on to his main thesis; but we will not pass on immediately, because the first examples which spring to mind are precisely those of the two men who are our theme.

Guénon was brought up as a Roman Catholic, and he ended up as a Muslim. Guénon was quite irregular, having said himself: "I am not a model to be followed in any way," because he had many different initiations: he had a Hindu initiation, a Taoist initiation, and finally an Islamic Sufi initiation, but it took him some time, because he was groping for his way.

In the case of Schuon, he was brought up as a Protestant in Germany, but his family had been Catholic, and his father, to whom he was extremely devoted and who died when Schuon was only thirteen years old, on his deathbed expressed the wish that his two sons should become Roman Catholics. Then they went to live in France, and after the First World War their country where they were born, which was in Germany, became part of France. So Schuon practised first of all Protestantism, and then he practised Roman Catholicism.

The reason for the change in both cases was the presence of a great spiritual master in the religion to which the change was made, and the absence of his counterpart in the other, the religion that was left. That was the only reason. In the case of Guénon—and one does not know this quite as well as what one knows about Schuon—but it must have been the man to whom he dedicated his book, *The Symbolism of the Cross*,[7] who was a great Egyptian shaykh of the *Shādhilī ṭarīqah*, and a spiritual authority even in exoteric Islam; whereas Frithjof Schuon became the disciple of the Shaykh al-ʿAlawī, the great Algerian Shaykh, who died I think it was in 1934; and in both cases there was no counterpart in the religion that was left. Yet there was also no "conversion". What Schuon means by that is that the religion that was left still continued to be loved and believed in.

But now we go back to the question of missionaries, and the title of the book, *The Transcendent Unity of Religions*, leads us to expect that from that title will come some remarks about missionaries, and we are not disappointed. I will just now give

[7] *Le symbolisme de la croix*, 1931, dedicated "To the revered memory of Shaykh ʿAbd al-Raḥmān ʿUlaysh al-Kabīr."

you what he says about the attempts to convert Hindus to Christianity:

> Brahmins are invited to abandon completely a religion that has lasted for several thousands of years, one that has provided the spiritual support of innumerable generations, and has produced flowers of wisdom and holiness down to our times. The arguments brought forward to justify this extraordinary demand are in no wise logically conclusive, nor do they bear any proportion to the magnitude of the demand. The reasons that the Brahmins have for remaining faithful to their spiritual patrimony are therefore infinitely stronger than the reasons by which it is sought to persuade them to cease being what they are. The disproportion, from the Hindu point of view, between the immense reality of the Brahmanic tradition and the insufficiency of the Christian counter-argument is such as to prove quite sufficiently that had God wished to submit the world to one religion only, the arguments put forward on behalf of this religion would not be so feeble, nor those of certain so-called infidels so powerful.

Equally unanswerable is Schuon's refutation of the claim that Islam is a pseudo-religion, which is the claim of the average Christian missionary:

> That God should have allowed a religion that was merely the invention of a man to conquer a part of humanity, and to maintain itself for more than a thousand years in a quarter of the inhabited world, thus betraying the love, faith, and hope of a multitude of sincere and fervent souls, this again is contrary to the laws of the divine Mercy, or in other words, to those of universal possibility.

He says elsewhere in the same passage, in the same sequence of thoughts: "God can be terrible, as the theologians well know, but he is not monstrous."

To that last passage one might say: "Yes, this is convincing, but nonetheless, great evil does exist in the world; how is that to be explained?" and in one of his other books Schuon does answer this question, I think, in the only possible way, and it is of very great importance. Of course, Sufism is identical with the Advaita Vedanta of Hinduism in its doctrine, and in the hierarchy of the universe both these esoterisms insist on the one divine Essence as being the Absolute, which Schuon defines further as Absolute-Infinite-Perfection. That is the divine Essence, and that, according to Sufism and Advaita Vedanta, is the sole Reality. The Hindus use the word *Atma*, and the term *Maya*, meaning "illusion," for all the rest. Even the Trinity is at the level of *Maya*, that is, the "illusion," since it is not at the highest level. This is what Meister Eckhart also believed, and many Christians have also insisted on this as well, but the official doctrine of both the Orthodox and the Catholic Church is that the Trinity is at the summit of the hierarchy. It is one God, and they insist on the unity of the Trinity, but nonetheless, the Hindus, who have also a Trinity in Hinduism, *Sat-Chit-Ananda*,[8] insist that that is not at the level of *Atma*, the Absolute, but that it is in the domain of illusion.

Now, in Sufism, some of the divine Names are Names of the Essence, and they are Names, therefore, of the Absolute; and one of these Names is the Name *al-Raḥmān*, which is translated in many different ways. It is one of the Names of Mercy. Schuon translates it "the Infinitely Good." It is one of the Names of the Essence, and it is through *al-Raḥmān*, the Infinitely Good, that the whole of creation—the whole of manifestation—takes place, because it is in the nature of the Good to radiate. This is a universal Truth which is recognised by Saint Augustine, for example, as well as Hindus and Muslims. There is a saying of the Prophet which is often quoted—some say it is not a saying of his, but it is nonetheless recognised as a truth: *I was a Hidden Treasure and I loved to be known, and so I created the world.*[9] This explains that the Sufi or Muslim point of view is exactly the same as that of the

[8] Being-Consciousness-Bliss. [9] See note 4, p. 83

Vedantist. They do not speak in Hinduism of creation, but of manifestation. The whole universe is a manifestation of God, of the Absolute; and radiation, which comes from the Good, means eventually distance, and distance produces danger. This is precisely the origin of all evil: it comes from the Infinitely Good, paradoxically speaking.

At a lower level, the personal God intervenes to control evil, to rectify it, but the personal God is all-powerful, except as regards the Essence. The God "the Law-Giver," "the Origin of all Justice," has power to correct evil, but He has no power to stop the radiation of Infinite Goodness which comes from the divine Essence, for He has no power over the divine Essence. He has power over everything else, so continually God intervenes in the world to stop evil. When one religion becomes defunct, He sends a new religion; when the religion of a community on Earth no longer operates, because man tends to drag things down always, then God sends, in His own time, a new religion. He is always intervening, but the flow of manifestation, the radiation which produces distance from which eventually evil comes, that cannot be stopped, because the divine nature cannot be changed, nor is it desirable that it should be changed. But that is why there is evil in the world. It is not due to any lack, anything that is missing in the Divinity. The correction of evil is there. The divine Justice is there, and penetrates the world, but It acts in Its own time. *A thousand years in Thy sight are but as yesterday.*[10] What seems to us a very long time, a very long period of tolerance by God, is really nothing.

Now, this is to do with the book *The Transcendent Unity of Religions*, which was the only book of Schuon's that Guénon read, and he had the highest praise for it, in particular for a chapter entitled "The Universality and Particular Nature of the Christian Tradition," which might be said to fill in some gaps left by Guénon. Or to take another of Schuon's books,

[10] Psalms 90:4.

Esoterism as Principle and as Way,[11] the title, which may be said to sum up its author's writings as a whole, can also be used to throw light on the difference between the providential functions of the two men we are speaking about. To sum up Guénon's output, the title in question would have to be changed to "Esoterism as Principle with a View to the Way." Guénon never lost sight of the Way, but he did not write about it directly, whereas Schuon did, and at least half his writings are about the Way. He was himself a spiritual master with many souls under his care, and Guénon did not have this function. This means that the writings of Schuon are rich in psychological observations of the utmost importance, and there is very little of any such thing in Guénon's writings. But one must remember that Guénon was the great pioneer. What Guénon did of immense value was to establish the hierarchy of the faculties in the world from the divine Truth Itself, that is, the Spirit, the Intellect—to restore to the word "intellect" its true meaning—and then the mind, sense and so on. Guénon re-established, for people who had forgotten it, the true meanings of various different words. But he did not make psychological observations.

Now, Jung once remarked, not without sagacity, that the soul is the object of modern psychology, but that unfortunately it is also the subject.[12] This amounts to a condemnation to the modern science in question. But in traditional civilisations, it was taken for granted that the soul can only be examined from a level higher than itself, that is, from a spiritual level. The priests in all traditional civilisations were the recognised authorities, and when Schuon speaks about the soul, we spontaneously accept what he says in the certitude that he is speaking from a level which transcends the psychic domain.

[11] First English edition by Perennial Books, 1981.

[12] C. G. Jung, *Psychology and Religion*, New Haven: Yale University Press, 1938, p. 62: "The object of psychology is the psychic; unfortunately it is

This will be thought not interesting to some people, but let me say in passing, that Schuon was remarkably aquiline in appearance, so much so that the Sioux Indians of North America, who adopted him into their tribe, would refer to his followers as the Eagle People, implying that Schuon himself was the Eagle. I mention this because one has the impression that, when he is speaking of the soul, he is looking down from above. This is very distinctive. Another point I would make is that after he had come to live in Indiana, he was visited every year by a Crow medicine man—another tribe of North American Indians—a man called Yellowtail, who has written a book which incidentally is of great interest. I think it is published by World Wisdom books in America, in Bloomington.[13] And Schuon once remarked to me that some people might find these regular visits, year after year, surprising, but he said the explanation is very simple: "Yellowtail is profoundly conscious of being a priest by his very nature, and he senses the same consciousness in me, despite the many outward differences between us."

To go back to the writings and to Schuon's function as a spiritual master, he demands, from the very start, total commitment to the Way: "Knowledge saves only on condition that it enlists all that we are. Metaphysical knowledge is sacred, and it is the right of sacred things to demand of man all that he is."[14] What is that "all?" The answer to this question is the theme of a chapter in *Esoterism as Principle and as Way* entitled "The Triple Nature of Man," and much of Schuon's other writings are concerned with this threefold totality. To sum up, it is a question of knowing, willing and loving the divine Reality. Since the Way demands perpetual consciousness of this triad, Schuon, for the easy remembrance of his disciples,

also its subject."

[13] Thomas Yellowtail, *Native Spirit: The Sun Dance Way*, recorded and edited by Michael Fitzgerald, Bloomington IN: World Wisdom, 2007.

[14] *Spiritual Perspectives and Human Facts*, Perennial Books, 1970, p. 138.

often words the triad "comprehension," "concentration" and "conformation." The faculties concerned are intelligence, will and sentiment, and this is related to another triad. Schuon defines the principles of the Way as Fear, Love and Knowledge, and this is something of universal import, and constitutes a whole. It is generally said in Islam that, provided that one fears God, one loves Him and one knows Him to the best of one's ability, He will ask nothing more of us. But this is really the same triad as the other one, because Will, the faculty of compulsion, is related to what must be done and what must be avoided. I stress the word "must," and danger is implicit in "must," and fear is implicit in danger, so that one can say that the three faculties, Will, Sentiment and Intelligence, are related to Fear, Love and Knowledge, which Schuon gives as the principles of the Path.

This is something which he insisted upon to the point of giving its applications to all sorts of things in life. For example, to take first of all this particular attitude of Fear, it is related to the virtue of sobriety, that is, not exaggerating, restraining oneself, abstaining from things. And this corresponds to the austerity of virgin nature. He always encouraged people to think of virgin nature as the natural setting for man, to feel at home, particularly, in virgin nature. Then he insisted on the importance of having a sanctuary in the house, if possible, as this was a traditional Sufi style, and since he was a Sufi, and his disciples were Sufis. This is for people living in the Western world, and it is extremely important—it was to be the centre of the house, and only used for prayer, and it must be in Islamic style and must reflect this particular attitude we are speaking of. It corresponded, as regards one's relationship with other people, to solitude, the first of those three things. In nature, this is the attitude of fear. One can use another word than "fear." If one likes, one can use the word "awe," awe of God, because God says to Moses in the Qur'ān: "Do not fear; My messengers are not afraid in my presence,"[15] but He does not say: "Do not have awe of Me." Primordial man lived without fear of God, but he lived in awe of God. So this first principle corresponds to what is usually called Fear.

The second principle is that of Love. As regards one's relationship with other spiritual men, Love corresponds to the spiritual festival. In virgin nature it corresponds to the beauty, or the splendour, of nature, and in the sanctuary it corresponds also to the element of splendour.

The third principle is Knowledge, and in nature this corresponds to the meaning, the symbolism of nature, the meaningful things of trees, rivers and flowers, and all that we see—the message they bear, if one likes. In the sanctuary it is the homogeneity of the sanctuary and also the meaning of the ornaments. The sanctuary must be meaningful. As regards one's relationship with others, it is the company of spiritual men, and Schuon adds: "All these things must be combined." This is essentially important, and is something which we find in all sacred art. Schuon was an artist—he was a painter and a poet—and it is very true; if one considers sacred art, all over the world, there are always these three elements which correspond to Awe, Love and Knowledge; a kind of austerity or simplicity, splendour and, of course, meaningfulness. And spiritually speaking, as part of a spiritual method, the other rooms in the house should, if possible, be like prolongations of the sanctuary. One should not put up ornaments which have no meaning; photographs of one's families, for example, were not allowed to be put upon the walls, because it was something too personal and not sufficiently meaningful, and not sufficiently beautiful in most cases. The question of beauty is extremely important.

This triad I am speaking of leads to something else, and to another of Schuon's books, called *Stations of Wisdom*,[16] because

15 Qur'ān, 27:10.

16 First published 1951.

each of these principles has two aspects. Where there is danger, there are two possibilities: flight or attack. Where there is Love, there are again two possibilities: there is a thankful repose in what one has, and there is a longing for what one has not yet been given. And then, as regards Knowledge, there is the objective knowledge of the Absolute-Infinite-Perfection viewed as an object, and there is the subjective consciousness that this is the object of gnosis, that is, Know Thyself, and that it is the true Self of each person. In his writings Schuon makes a great deal of what he calls "the miracle of subjectivity," a very remarkable thing which people take for granted. But everybody knows that he is "I," and that is an extraordinary thing. This is because the divine Self is One, and that Oneness radiates even into the world. Everyone knows that, but Schuon is possibly one of the first writers to make a great deal of that point, which he calls "the miracle of subjectivity." It is a letting out of a secret on an immense scale, on a universal scale. There is something really wonderful about that, that everybody knows that he is "I."

Each of these three principles of the triad has two aspects, and this produces six principles which Schuon calls "the stations of wisdom"—the six stations of wisdom. This is a very important point of universal doctrine. At the Fall of Man, the greater, outer world—the macrocosm—did not fall. It is only Man, the microcosm, that fell. The macrocosm retained its primordial perfection, with its six dimensions remaining in all the fullness that they were: the North, South, East and West, height and depth. Now, man, the microcosm, like the macrocosm, was created in the image of God, and has also these six dimensions, and these are precisely the six principles which I have just been speaking of. They correspond precisely in the outer world to the directions of space, and man has to restore to these directions their fullness. To the North corresponds the aspect of Fear or danger; it is the cold station, the station symbolised by crystal, by ice, by snow, and relates to purity; it corresponds to death in the cycle of Man's life; it corresponds to the season of winter; and it corresponds to taking refuge from the world, that is, fleeing danger, which is what we fear. Whereas the other aspect of Fear corresponds to what is called in Islam the Greater Holy War, the fighting against the danger and putting an end to it. When the Prophet was returning from the victory over Mecca, he said: *We have returned from the lesser holy war to the greater holy war.* And when asked what that was, he said: *It is the war against the soul.* Therefore, the greater holy war is the war against the soul, and that corresponds to the East, and to youth and vigour in the cycle of Man's life

Then there are the two aspects of Love: the grateful repose in what one has received corresponds to the West, that is, the complement of the East, and it corresponds to the beginning of old age in life, when one looks back in gratitude to all that one has received.

The South, corresponding to summer, is the complement of winter. As Schuon has said, the first station of wisdom says "No" to the world. The fourth station of wisdom—its complement which corresponds to summer—says "Yes" to God.

The height and depth correspond to the two aspects of Knowledge. The height is the transcendent Object, and the depth is the immanent Self, that is, the Subject, and these six stations of wisdom are the theme of the last chapter of Schuon's book of that title, *The Stations of Wisdom*. And it is that that has to be gained. The soul has to regain its six dimensions in full: its North, South, East and West in full as they were.

Another thing I might just mention connected with the psychology is this: I read fairly recently a remark in some journal or other: "We hear that Frithjof Schuon believes in the caste system, and this tells us that none of his books can be worth reading." Indeed, Schuon has written a book called *Castes and Races*,[17] and I would say it is one of the most delightful of his books to read, because it is very easy to read and it is of extraordinary interest. He speaks first of all about the castes and explains their meaning and nature, defining each of the four castes very thoroughly. He points out that Hinduism has retained its vigour because of the caste system, which has protected the Hindu tradition from degenerating. Its sister traditions of Greece and Rome, belonging to the same age as Hinduism, have come to nothing. Hinduism is still fully alive and fully operative, and that can only be explained by the caste system.

Schuon points out that caste is a reality, but that the class a person may belong to is something purely artificial. In Hinduism the two things coincided, but caste itself is something which is real, and a man in the modern Western world is nearly always a mixture, a combination of *Kshatriya* and *Vaisha*, or possibly *Brahmin* and *vaisha*, or *Brahmin* and *Kshatriya*. Seldom in the world has the caste system never existed, and it is seldom that the pure caste manifests itself. It is always a possibility, but it is very seldom, but it is nonetheless a reality. He then writes about the races, and it is wonderful to read what he says about each of the three races, their particular aptitudes, their particular gifts, and so on. I will just suggest that the book should be read with interest.

But now, in conclusion, I will just quote something, an example from his book *Islam and the Perennial Philosophy*,[18] which illustrates his extraordinary perceptivity and his subtlety in seeing situations, and this is about the modern world. I have quoted some of it before, but not as much as this. In his writings, like Guénon, Schuon is, of course, very much against the idea of "progress," that man is progressing, and, of course, totally against the idea of evolution. In the last half of the century it is so obvious that man is not getting better and better, but he says here:

---

[17] First published by Perennial Books, 1959. [18] First published 1976.

> It must be admitted that the progressists [those who believe in progress] are not entirely wrong in thinking that there is something in religion which no longer works. In fact the individualistic and sentimental argumentation with which traditional piety operates has lost almost all its power to pierce consciences, and the reason for this is not merely that modern man is irreligious, but also that the usual religious arguments, through not probing sufficiently to the depth of things, and not having had previously any need to do so, are psychologically somewhat outworn, and fail to satisfy certain needs of causality. If human societies degenerate, on the one hand, with the passage of time, they accumulate, on the other hand, experiences in virtue of old age, however intermingled with errors their experiences may be. This paradox is something that any pastoral teaching bent on efficacy should take into account, not by drawing new directives from the general error, but on the contrary, by using arguments of a higher order, intellectual rather than sentimental. As a result, some at least would be saved, a greater number than one might be tempted to suppose, whereas the demagogic scientistic pastoralist saves no one.

By that last phrase, "the demagogic scientistic pastoralist," he is no doubt thinking of those who put forward Vatican II, who are bent on modernising the Church, making people feel at home in religion, and so on.

But another point in another book, which he makes in connection with this, is about men having a certain experience, and there being a certain wisdom of old age in the air. There is no doubt about that, and I think he is the first person to mention this, but in a chapter called "Understanding and Believing" in his book *Logic and Transcendence*,[19] he points out that it is well accepted that it is possible to believe without understanding. One of the great English saints, Saint

[19] First English edition, 1975.

Anselm, said: *Credo ut intelligam*, "I believe in order that I may understand," and that is a certain relationship which is effective, but Schuon points out that in the modern world it is unfortunately the other way round; there is understanding without believing, and that is something very typical of the modern world, and that rather lessens the efficacy of old age. There is a lot of old age, a certain experience of old age, which is a certain wisdom, but which is nonetheless weakened by the fact that many people understand things but they no longer believe; they no longer have faith in religion.

I think I will just end my talk with an example of Schuon's gift for expressing something in a very concentrated form. It was, no doubt, with his disciples in view, but it also is a general principle. This is an unpublished text which he called "The Chain of Quintessences." He begins: "The quintessence of the world is Man," for Man is the centre of the worldly state, of course, and all tradition is in agreement about that. He expresses it like this:

> The quintessence of the world is Man. The quintessence of Man is religion. The quintessence of religion is prayer. The quintessence of prayer is invoking the Name of God. If man had no more than a few instants to live, he would no longer be able to do anything but invoke God. He would thereby fulfil all the demands of prayer, of religion, of the human state.

In a certain sense it is always a death to remember what is transcendent in this life, and I will read you just another short passage which was published in a little anthology, one of the last things to be published, *Echoes of Perennial Wisdom*:[20]

> There are two moments in life which are everything, and these are the present moment, when we are free to choose what we would be, and the moment of death, when we have no longer any choice, and the decision belongs to

20 Bloomington IN: World Wisdom, 1992.

God. Now, if the present moment is good, death will be good. If we are now with God in this present, which is ceaselessly being renewed, but which remains always this one and only moment of actuality, God will be with us at the moment of death. The remembrance of God is a death in life. It will be a life in death.

Human Origins and Destinies according to the Great Religions of the World

LADIES AND GENTLEMEN, we might ask the question, seeing that I am speaking about human origins and human destinies according to the great religions of the world: "What does religion mean?" and if we look at the word, it is a question of restoring the ligament—the syllable *lig* in "religion"—the bond between God and man. That is in danger of being forgotten in the modern world. And one of the first things to be considered is that here below the material world seems to be the most real of all things. It is almost proverbial that appearances are deceptive, and that is true in the sense of the material world. The soul is also real because we are conscious of it, but all beyond that is considered today by many people to be questionable, and even improbable.

But man was created with the certitude that the invisible beyond is in fact supreme Reality. There is a saying in Islam, which is clearly one of those sayings of the Prophet where God speaks in the first person upon his tongue—which is very relevant to our talk—and I have often quoted it before: *I was a hidden treasure and I loved to be known, and so I created the world.*

This can be applied, and clearly does apply, to both the macrocosm and the microcosm, that is, the great outer world and the small world of man; both are made in the image of God, and both exist in order that the Hidden Treasure may be known. How can we define the Hidden Treasure Itself? We would have to use many words, but it is sometimes summed up in the words: "Absolute-Infinite-Eternal Perfection." One could say: "Absolute-Infinite-Beauty-Reality-Wisdom-Happiness-Goodness-Unity."

In the modern world one often hears the words spoken: "How can I believe in a God who allows such evil to exist?" Again and again in my life I have heard those words, or not exactly the same words, but the same thought expressed, and it is often summed up as the so-called "problem of evil." The answer to this question: "How are we to understand the existence of evil?" has been answered by Frithjof Schuon, whom I would say if I were asked—at least it is my opinion—that he is the greatest writer of the last century, and I have not read any better explanation of evil than what he himself wrote: "It is in the nature of the Good to radiate."[1] That is one of the essential aspects of Goodness.

Now, radiation produces distance, and distance is, of course, a dangerous thing. God is All-Powerful, but His All-Power, His Omnipotence, is not at the level of the Hidden Treasure itself, and it has no power over the Hidden Treasure. I repeat, it is in the nature of the Good to radiate; the divine Omnipotence can stop everything which is below the level of the Hidden Treasure, but it cannot prevent Goodness from radiating. The Infinite, Eternal Goodness of God radiates, and His Omnipotence is continually intervening to correct the Good in the face of the dangers which spring ultimately from distance.

You have in the Book of Genesis the words: *The Spirit of God breathed upon the face of the waters... and the waters were divided.*[2] Hinduism has also the doctrine of the two waters: the upper waters and the lower waters. Just the same we find in Islam; the Qur'ān mentions the two seas, one sweet and fresh, the

[1] See "The Mystery of the Veil" in *Esoterism as Principle and as Way*, and "The Quintessential Esoterism of Islam" in *Sufism: Veil and Quintessence*.
[2] Genesis 1:2 and 6.

other salt and bitter.[3] Now this other, the salt and bitter, is the world we live in, the lower waters; but the upper waters are the domain of the hierarchy of the Paradises, what we call Heaven—all belong to the upper waters, and they are too near to God for the existence of evil to be possible. But in this world, which the words "lower waters" refer to, distance makes evil a possibility, though the divine Omnipotence is continually intervening—hence the existence of religion—to reduce and correct the evil.

In the Christian Middle Ages, and an equivalent could be found in other traditions, students were taught that man has four faculties. I think this teaching was taken originally from Boethius.[4] The four faculties are: Intellect, which is concerned with the realities of the next world; Reason, which is concerned with this world, and which is under the guidance of the Intellect; Imagination is under the same guidance; and the fourth faculty is that of Sense, that is, the five senses, and they are the meeting place of soul and body. It is almost impossible to say exactly where the soul ends and where the body begins, or the other way round.

It is the Intellect which Meister Eckhart defined as being uncreated and uncreatable.[5] Modern man has retained the word on account of its high-sounding nature, but has lost sight of its meaning altogether, and if we hear someone described as one of the leading intellectuals of our day, it is probable that the person in question will be, in fact, anti-intellectual, that is, not believing that the next world exists.

To come back to true meanings, what is known by the esoterists, the mystics of all religions, as the Heart, if they are not simply referring to the bodily heart, is the centre of the soul. A centre is always higher than the rest of its domain, being like a door that opens onto a higher world. In this sense, it could be said that the Heart is between the two seas, and the Heart is thus sometimes said to be the Throne of the Intellect.

---

[3] Qur'ān 25:53. [4] See *The Consolation of Philosophy*, V. [5] Sermon 24.

Thus the word "heart" as it is used in spiritual writings can be used analogously at higher levels, as a gateway, as an opening from one world to another.

One of the poems of the great Sufi, that is, the Islamic mystic, Al-Ḥallāj, whom you may have heard of, begins: *I saw my Lord with the eye of the heart; I said: "Who art Thou?" He answered "Thou,"*[6] and in that case the word "heart" is used in a higher level. But in its normal use the word "intuition" could be used for what lies between the mind, where the faculty of reason works, and the Intellect, to which it leads—one could say that it belongs to the higher reaches of the human intelligence, between the mind and the Heart.

It is access to the Heart that was lost at the Fall of Man. When the Fall of Man is spoken of, it means loss of access to the Heart. In all traditions, Man is the representative of God on Earth, made in His image, and Man is the centre of the earthly plane. In the biblical account of the Creation, Man, made in the image of God, is the last to be created, and it is interesting to note that the letter *waw*, which expresses Man's function as mediator between Heaven and Earth, in both Arabic and Hebrew has the value of six, precisely, that is, the linguistic mediator has the value of six, the number of the day on which Man was created. When I say "the linguistic mediator" I mean the word "and," which in both Arabic and Hebrew is written with one letter which has the value of six, because the letters in sacred languages, like Arabic and Hebrew, have numerical values, and it is significant that Man, the mediator between Heaven and Earth, was created on the sixth day. Seven, of course, is a divine number.

Now, having spoken a little about human origins, I think it is time I came to the question of human destinies. The religions are concerned with guiding man back to his origin; that is the purpose of religion: to lead man back to his

---

[6] Abū Bakr Sirāj al-Dīn, *The Book of Certainty: The Sufi Doctrine of Faith, Vision and Gnosis*, Cambridge: Islamic Texts Society, 1992.

origin in the Hidden Treasure. Owing to the Fall of Man, this return requires that we should regain the perfection which Man had at his creation and which was lost at the Fall, and in all religions one can find the equivalent of what in the Christian world were called the Lesser Mysteries and the Greater Mysteries. The Lesser Mysteries are concerned with purification, that is, they are concerned with regaining the state of human perfection in which Man was created; the Greater Mysteries are concerned with the return to God, the return to the Hidden Treasure from which Man came.

If we take the great poem of Dante, *The Divine Comedy*, we know that it is divided into three parts, the *Inferno*, the *Purgatorio* and the *Paradiso*. The Inferno and the Purgatory belong to the Lesser Mysteries; the third book of Dante's poem, the Paradise, belongs to the Greater Mysteries. And one finds in all religions the equivalent of Hell and of Purgatory. In the case of Dante's poem, his descent into Hell signifies a coming to know of one's own faults, and it is, in a sense, simultaneous with Purgatory, which is the purification from faults. The two together make up the Lesser Mysteries, as I have said, and the Greater Mysteries are the ascent through the different celestial degrees to the ultimate end of all things, which is the Hidden Treasure itself.

But what of those who have lost their religion, and have lost belief in religious teaching? I am told that one sees in some of the cities of the modern world, in certain places, where criminals make a point of living in certain communities of criminals; one sees boys of seven with faces of men of forty. They have been brought up from their earliest infancy on the principle: "Get what you can, how you can, when you can," with no question of any religion taught them at all. What are we to think of this in relation to the goodness of God? where is the justice of God ? In answering this question we must understand that in the older religions—Hinduism and Buddhism, for example—there is the doctrine of the *samsara*.

The macrocosm can be likened to the circumference of a circle, and the different religions could be looked at as points on this circumference. Each of these points has a radius which leads to the centre, the centre being the Hidden Treasure itself, but the points on the circumference correspond to the outer aspect of religion, and religions are often seen to disagree with one another at this level. But the radius which attaches each of the points to the centre is the inner aspect of religion, that domain which is referred to by us in English as mysticism, and the nearer the radii get to the centre, the nearer the religions come to each other.

Now, there are many Christians, since the time of the so-called Reformation, who have cancelled out the idea of Purgatory altogether, because they say that it is not mentioned in the Bible. I was brought up myself as an Anglican, and rather a Low Church Anglican, which meant that I was told that there is no such thing as Purgatory, that either one goes to Heaven or to Hell at one's death. I was taught that it is no good even praying for the dead, because either they are in Heaven, in which case they do not need your prayers, or they are in Hell and it is too late to pray for them. But that did not satisfy me. In consequence, I never stopped praying, but I did stop attending the Anglican church where I was taken unwillingly as a child.

But now we are speaking of these things, it is important to mention this: in the early Middle Ages, Saint Ireneus pronounced it to be a heresy to believe that salvation was the equivalent of supreme spiritual realisation, that is, was the equivalent of sanctity, and all religions are in agreement with that. This means that the person who has salvation does not necessarily go straight to Heaven, to Paradise, at death, but that he is saved from passing out of this world and losing his central position, and becoming at the level of lower beings which are not central, which are animal, or even still lower than that.

There is in Buddhism a very beautiful image of a waiting-place at the edge of Paradise, where souls have to prepare themselves. Even if they have gone through the process of Purgatory, they still cannot be necessarily ripe to enter Paradise itself, and in Buddhism they use the image of a lotus bud: the soul is placed in a lotus bud where it matures, and in which it has no longer anything to suffer; but it longs to enter Paradise and it is not yet ready. As it becomes ready, the petals of the lotus gradually open, and finally the soul is set free and able to enter Paradise. And one finds this doctrine of the waiting-place in all the religions. In Islam, for example, one of the chapters of the Qur'ān is called "The Heights", and one reads in this chapter that on the Heights are men who have not yet entered Paradise, though they long to do so,[7] and that waiting-place is equivalent to the Buddhist lotus bud. It is generally understood that only the saints enter Paradise directly after death. Other people who are saved, they have attained salvation, but they have to be ready to enter Paradise, and this can easily be understood. To be in Paradise is clearly a great responsibility—and this applies to all religions—because one of the greatest blessings of Paradise consists of the saints themselves who are in Paradise, and it is necessary that there is enough human maturity to enter Paradise. It means that the soul in question must be capable of being a source of delight to all the other souls in Paradise. That is a tremendous responsibility, and that is why salvation does not mean beatification, but it means that it will come—it is a kind of promise that Paradise will come. It is only that what I have just said is not mentioned in the New Testament, and it is rejected by many people who say that either one is in Hell or one is in Paradise and, in consequence, there is no need to pray for the dead.

In speaking of our human ends, I thought that I could end this talk with a poem which I wrote on this subject of the great

[7] *Al-Aʿrāf*, 7:46.

religions. So if you will bear with me, I will just read this poem, and it is called *Requiem*:

Hindus relinquish not their belovèd in death,
But year after year, from youth to age,
Help them with offerings to the Holy Fire,
Kindled on the altar, to Agni, the Lord,
Who purifies and transmutes; and to the priest, bountifully,
The rich man of his gold gives, or of cattle,
And the poor what he may of milk and of fruit,
Certain that these offerings the after-life will reach,
Following the departed, not in form, but in Spirit,
For a gift sanctified by sacrifice has wings.
And they pray: From the bond of rebirth and redeath
Liberate them with Knowledge of none but Thee,
O Truth, O Self of their selves, O Peace.

Jews make studies of their Sacred Books,
Dedicating those studies to dead kinsmen—
Theirs be the merits and the meed!—and alms
They give that their sins be forgiven, to the Lord
Praying at Passover, Pentecost, Atonement
And Tabernacles—some every Sabbath, every day—
That their dead He may bless and bring into the serene
Paradise of Abraham, Isaac and Jacob
Sheltered forever beneath the shadow of his wings.

The Buddhists of the North and the Buddhists of the South
Deeds of excellence to their dead transfer,
And two vessels they take, one full,
Empty the other, and the empty they fill,
Pouring in water for witnesses to see,
Symbol of the giving and seal upon the gift,
Pouring water, pouring virtue,
Gravity celestial, from the living to the dead,

To increase what store they acquired in life,
That the world's gravity be outweighed, and they drawn
From the rim of the immense round of existences,
Wheel of vicissitude, that to the Centre they may attain.

The Churches of the East, and the Church of the West,
Their memorial stones with reminders engrave
For passers-by to pray for the dead.
The bereaved solemnate requiems and vigils,
And offerings make for remission of sins,
And light candles, and litanies recite:
Kyrie eleison, Christe eleison,
Kyrie eleison: thus the living for the dead,
Pray to the Merciful that His Mercy may save
And bring their souls to the bliss of Heaven.
And they beseech Mary, beseech Michael,
And all Angels, and all the Saints,
To cry with them: *Kyrie eleison,*
Christe eleison, Kyrie eleison.

Muslims mention with Mercy their dead,
They utter not their names without utterance of a prayer,
And they pray, standing or sitting, at their tombs,
Fasts for their salvation and vigils they keep,
And chant the Qur'ān, and charities bestow.
For the dead Mecca and Medina they visit,
Jerusalem, or shrine of Saint, dedicating
The Pilgrimage to them—theirs be the Blessing!
And together in Mosques in congregation they pray
Alike for the dead as for the living, and invoke
The All-Merciful: have Mercy upon us.

Could these, and these, and these be wrong,
And these and these? Could they be wrong,
And ye be right, ye right alone,
Sects that pray not for departed souls?
Shalt thou, and thou, and thou the gates

Enter of Paradise, only for being
Not bad enough to burn in Hell?
Gladdeners of the enemy, ye glut him with two feasts:
Living complacence; and prayers filched
From the derelict dead in their direst need.

Church Triumphant and Church Militant,
For the Church Suffering, O intercede, and pray
For Mercy on the dead: On the dead, Mercy!

Islam: an Introduction

My talk was given out as *Islam: an Introduction*, and I was overawed when I read the announcement, because it is a tremendous subject to deal with in just one lecture. So I must not waste any time. I think many of you are Muslims, but for those who are not, I must give them the introduction promised them, and I must therefore begin by pointing out that Islam is based on the Qur'ān, which is direct Revelation like the Pentateuch—that is, the first five books of the Old Testament which are known in Islam as the Torah—and the Psalms, whereas the rest of the Old Testament—the Book of Kings, the Book of Chronicles and so forth—are not Revelation at all; they are, one might say, inspired sacred history composed and written down by men, perhaps under inspiration. The same applies to the New Testament. In Christianity it is Christ Himself, "the Word made Flesh" as the Christians say, who holds the central place which is held in Islam by "the Word made Book," that is, the Qur'ān. And instead of calling Islam "Muhammadanism," as happened throughout the centuries until recently, it would have been reasonable to call it "Qur'ānism"; but there was no question of that, because the Qur'ān itself says that God has chosen to name the religion *Islām*, which means "submission to God."

The Qur'ān is the book of God in more than one sense: it is from God, it is mainly about God, and above all, it is of one substance with God, that is, it is not created. It is also—and has been called very often—the Book of Truth. And it is sometimes said that Islam is a religion of Truth, unlike

Christianity which is a religion of Love. But, of course, there must always be the element Love and there must always be the element Truth; it is a question simply of emphasis between these two religions. One could also name the Qur'ān "the Book of Mercy," because Mercy is one of its main themes, and every chapter but one begins with the *Basmalah*, that is, *In the Name of God, the Infinitely Good, the Boundlessly Merciful.* One could also, by extension, name the Qur'ān "the Book of Paradise," because there is so much in the book about Paradise. But Mercy and Paradise will form one of the main themes of my second talk, so that I will not say now anything more about that aspect of Islam.

I will now invite you to take a plunge, as it were, into Islam by joining me in a point of view which, while being both un-Jewish and un-Christian, is essentially Islamic, although it is not typical of Muslims, for it eludes the majority. Nonetheless, the religion of Islam clearly offers it, whereas the Jew or Christian who adopt this point of view are compelled to step outside the framework of their religions. To explain this point of view, I must first say that the Qur'ān stresses the beauty of the Names of God, and it is generally said that they are ninety-nine in number, which must not be taken in any sense as a limitation, because it is simply a symbolic number which must be taken as expressive of the divine infinitude. One of these Names is *al-Badīʿ*, which is difficult to translate, but could be given as "the Marvellously Original," and one of the features of the Qur'ān is that it impels us to take notice of, to meditate on and to venerate what it calls the Signs of God.[1] The word *āyāt*,[2] which this translates, is also difficult to interpret: one could say "signs," "tokens"; but by "signs" we mean here signs of God's work in the Universe—outstanding things which take us back to God as their Archetype. And among the great Signs of God are His different religions. Other Signs which the Qur'ān mentions—and this is something that we do not find in either

[1] For one among many examples, cf. 27:93. [2] Sing. *āyah*.

the Jewish or the Christian books—is mention of the marvels of nature as among His Signs, insisting that we take note of them and meditate upon them. The element "miracle" in Islam is not lacking, because the Prophet performed many miracles, but they were never allowed to take the centre of the stage as they do in both Judaism and in Christianity. The great miracle is the Qur'ān itself and the world as it is, and which men have come to take for granted. The Qur'ān exclaims at one moment: *Will they not behold the camels, how they are created; and the firmament, how it is raised aloft; and the mountains, how they are established; and the earth, how it is spread?*[3]

Those verses are altogether typical of the Qur'ān, and you see what I meant by saying that you do not find such verses in general in the Old Testament, and not often in the Gospel, with the exception of the wonderful passage when Jesus says: *Consider the lilies of the field, how they grow; they toil not, neither do they spin; and yet I say unto you that even Solomon in all his glory was not arrayed like one of these.*[4] That is a passage in the New Testament to which every Muslim would take to spontaneously. But the Qur'ān is full of such passages.

Apart from nature, among the great signs are His Messengers and Prophets, and His religions. The Qur'ān continually speaks of different prophets and different religions. I should perhaps explain that the word "Messenger" translates the Arabic *rasūl*, which is the highest degree of prophethood, that is the founder of religion. The first of all the great *rusul*[5]—the great Messengers—is Adam. Although the Islamic doctrine is exactly the same as regards the Fall of Man as the Christian and Jewish doctrines, yet unlike Christianity, the Qur'ān tells us that God forgave Adam and sent him the first religion, so that Adam is above all in Islam one of the great divine Messengers, who brought the first religion to mankind. I will not mention them all, but then Noah, Abraham, Moses, Jesus and Muḥammad are among the great Messengers. Whereas the

[3] 88:17–20. [4] St Luke, 12:27. [5] Pl. of *rasūl*.

Prophets are David, Solomon, Aaron, Joseph—and many others are mentioned in the Qur'ān—and those are at a lesser degree of greatness than the Messengers themselves. These are themes within the Qur'ān, and we are told to marvel at these Messengers and at the religions that they founded, and we see here the function of the Qur'ān, or the function of Islam as the last religion, being necessarily something of a summing up of things.

We are given in the Qur'ān a vast perspective, and not content with what it says about the various Messengers and Prophets, it says in one verse, addressing the Prophet Muḥammad, *We have sent messengers before thee; about some of them We have told thee, and about some We have not told thee.*[6] It says also, *For every community there is a messenger.*[7] To mention this was a necessity, because if we read the Old Testament and then the New Testament we find practically nothing about other religions, and we wonder, "What about the rest of the world?—were they left in darkness?" The Qur'ān gives very clearly that answer, and I was asked once by a Turkish lady, did I think that the Buddha was one of the Messengers that the Qur'ān refers to who is not mentioned in the Qur'ān. And I said, yes. I think we must conclude that, because Buddhism has dominated for over two thousand years the whole of the Far East, despite a certain amount of Christian and Islamic penetration, and God would not have allowed that if the Buddha had not been one of the Messengers. And if he were not one of the Messengers, who was the Messenger that God sent? because the Qur'ān tells us, *For every community a Messenger has been sent.* So we are given here a vast panorama, an immense vista, which is, as I repeat, one of the aspects of Islam being the last religion of this cycle of time, and therefore something of a summing up.

For those of you who are not Muslims, I must give you something about the structure of Islam. And I cannot do

[6] 40:78 [7] 10:47

better, I think, than refer to that great occasion when the Archangel Gabriel appeared, not only to the Prophet, as he did frequently—and normally speaking the Prophet was the only one who could see him, and he was invisible to everybody else—but on this occasion he appeared to everybody who happened to be with the Prophet at that time; and he asked the Prophet three questions—that is, he asked him more than three questions, but I will deal with three questions.

What is the surrender? that is, what is *islām*? And the Prophet replied, *That thou shouldst testify that there is no god but God, and that Muḥammad is God's Messenger; that thou shouldst perform the prayer, bestow the alms, fast Ramadan, and make if thou canst the Pilgrimage to the Holy House*, that is, to Mecca. Then he said, *What is faith* (īmān)? And the Prophet answered, *It is that thou shouldst believe in God, and His Angels, and His Books, and His Messengers, and the Last Day; and that thou shouldst believe that no good or evil cometh but by His Providence.* And then the Angel asked, *What is excellence?* that is, *iḥsān* in Arabic. And the Prophet replied, *It is that thou shouldst worship God as if thou sawest Him; for if thou seest Him not, verily He seeth thee.*[8]

Now, *excellence* is associated with mysticism, because that degree of concentration demanded, *that thou shouldst worship God as if thou sawest Him*, is something that cannot be demanded of a majority of people. This will be one of the main themes of my third talk, so I will say no more about that. But these three questions are authoritative, because after the Angel had left, the Prophet asked one of his companions, *Did you know who the questioner was?* and he replied, no. And he said, *It was Gabriel; he came to teach you your religion.* So that these three questions and the answers given are of fundamental importance.

I should mention again, just in connection with the immense vista of Islam, that the Qur'ān gives that creed in

---

[8] According to a hadith (a saying of the Prophet) recorded by Muslim and Nawawī.

one verse, that the believers *believe in God, and His angels, and His Books, and His messengers; We make no distinction between His messengers*.[9] And it is a characteristic of Islam that you will find a tremendous veneration for all the Prophets, and above all, for the Messengers. In Christianity one does not find that, and one does not find that in Judaism, because there is not so much mention of the Prophets; but in Islam one finds a very great veneration and love for Prophets such as Aaron, for example—who means practically nothing to the average Christian—Joseph, David, Solomon. David and Solomon are counted as Prophets in Islam; in Judaism they are kings of Israel, they are not counted as Prophets. And of course Zachariah, John the Baptist—they are among the Prophets who are venerated in Islam.

Another point I would like to mention in connection with this immensity of the perspective which is not only in space but also in time. One of the conditions of Islam, you remember, is the pilgrimage to the Holy House, if one can do that. The pilgrimage to the *Kaʿba*, which was built by Abraham, is an Abrahamic rite which is taken into Islam. It is an amazing experience to make the pilgrimage for almost every Muslim when they do that, and I have heard people say that this is not the Islam that I know. It is something quite outside everyone's experience until they make it, and when one goes to Mecca on the pilgrimage one has the impression that one is back in the time of Abraham. You see the people in their pilgrim dress going backwards and forwards between the two hills, as Hagar did when she was looking for water for Ishmael, who was lying in the sand, for whom God made a spring of water spout up in the sand—which is named the Well of Zamzam—near to which Abraham and Ishmael built by the order of God the *Kaʿba*, that is, the almost cubic-shaped House which is the centre of the Islamic world, and towards which the prayer is made.

---

[9] 2:285

When one performs the pilgrimage one is back in the far past. This rite is a pre-Mosaic rite. Judaism only came into existence with the Revelation on Mount Sinai to Moses. The Qur'ān insists that Abraham was neither a Christian nor a Jew—he was a *ḥanīf*,[10] which means an orthodox worshipper, and the nearest people to Abraham are the Muslims. And parallel to this dimension of Islam—the pilgrimage—going right back into far antiquity, is the fact that the Arabic language itself is wonderfully archaic. It is much more archaic than the Hebrew of Moses, which is another Semitic language, of course.

As the last Revelation, the Qur'ān gives answers to various things which are relevant to the age in which we live, and it gives answers to questions which have been raised only in recent times about other religions. I referred to Solomon just now, and you probably know that in the Old Testament, in the Book of Kings or Chronicles—which are not Revelation, they are sacred history written down by men—Solomon is given a bad report. It is a very peculiar state of affairs, because on the one hand Solomon is known throughout the world as the personification of Wisdom: "As wise as Solomon"—one finds that phrase in every European language, I think; and in Jewish mysticism he is known as the Father of the Cabbala. But nonetheless, the Book of Kings says, *And Solomon did evil in the sight of the Lord, and he was not as his father David.*[11]

But the Qur'ān re-establishes Solomon as a great Prophet without any reservations whatsoever, so that in Islam Solomon is venerated among the greatest of the Prophets. Another point—and it is only today that the question is disputed by people who can really be called heretics from a Christian point of view—is the virgin birth of Jesus. No Muslim will accept anything other than the virgin birth of Jesus. It is in the Qur'ān, and there is no doubt in the mind of any Muslim about that, whereas today certain Christians, so called,

---

10 3:67 11 I Kings, 11:6.

are beginning to question that point. Even the Immaculate Conception of the Virgin is in the Qur'ān, because while she was still in her mother's womb, her mother dedicated her to God and took refuge for her from Satan.[12] And the Prophet himself said, *Satan toucheth every son of Adam the day his mother beareth him, save only Mary and her son.*[13] That is an example of certain points that the Qur'ān makes absolutely clear.

Another thing I should mention is this: there is a considerable anticipation in the Qur'ān of various errors—of various particularly modern errors. For example, it should be impossible for a Muslim to believe in progress, human progress as it is portrayed. I was brought up on progress when I was young. All the teachers at my school believed that the First World War was the war to end all wars, and that the Earth would now progress, go on progressing, that it had progressed, and all the different modern inventions were the signs of progress. Now the Qur'ān is quite explicit: that the passage of time always produces the contrary of progress. The Prophet said, for example, *No time cometh upon you but is followed by a worse.*[14] He said also, *The best of my people are my generation, then those that come after them, then those that come after those.*[15] And there are many other passages in the Qur'ān and in the sayings of the Prophet which express the same idea. There is a verse in the Qur'ān referring to a certain people, of which the meaning is: *A long time passed over them, so that their hearts were hardened,*[16] meaning that the inevitable result of the passage of time is the hardening of hearts. This of course cannot possibly be taken as what one might call pessimism; it is just realism. But at the same time, God is always setting things right when they go wrong, and the Prophet said that God will send at the end of every hundred years a "renewer" who will renew His religion.[17] But that does not mean that the flow of decadence is stopped; it means that a certain rectification takes place, but

[12] 3:35 [13] Hadith recorded by Muslim. [14] Hadith recorded by Bukhārī. [15] Bukhārī. [16] 57:16 [17] Recorded by Abū Dā'ūd.

the flow goes on to the end of time, to the end of the cycle, until God will intervene again. All general betterment is made, according to Islam, by divine intervention against the process of descent which is the fatal characteristic of the human race.

The other great error of modern times is, of course, the belief in evolution. That is beginning to be questioned by scientists, but here again the Qur'ān is quite clear. The Bible as well is absolutely explicit. One cannot say the Qur'ān is more explicit than the Bible, but people in the West have ceased to take the Bible altogether seriously, whereas every Muslim takes the story of the creation of Adam *in perfect rectitude*, as the Qur'ān says, as something which is absolutely to be believed in, and it is impossible to believe in the idea that man is descended from anything else. Man was created last of all beings *in the most perfect rectitude*—to use the words of the Qur'ān: *fī aḥsani taqwīm—then We cast him down to be the lowest of the low*,[18] because man has become, according to the Qur'ān, worse than the animals—the worst of mankind[19] are further astray than the animals, who are at least innocent.

To go back to the question of other religions, one thing that the Muslim cannot help noticing—and this goes back to the divine Name *al-Badīʿ*, "the Marvellously Original"—is that the difference between the great Messengers and the religions they found is something overwhelming. Let us consider simply the difference between the two last religions. The extraordinary complementarity between a religion founded by a man with no earthly father—as the Qur'ān says, *The Word of God Whom He cast unto Mary, and a Spirit from God*[20]—one who stands above the world, scarcely entering into the world, and who performs miracle after miracle, some of outstanding magnitude, and a religion founded by a man who was plunged as deeply as possible into this world as regards human experiences, having been orphaned of a father before birth, and of his mother at the age of six, but blessed with a loving grandfather and uncle,

[18] 95:4–5 [19] 8:55 [20] 4:171

for many years husband of one wife fifteen years older than himself, and then for many years the husband of many wives, some much younger, and all much younger than himself, and in the world a man who was shepherd, merchant, then exile, Prophet, king, general, all to perfection. And on these two complementary perfections the two religions in question still live and draw their sustenance, one might say. One could take other religions also and compare them. All these religions are among the great Signs of God which the Qur'ān insists that we shall take into account and meditate on.

One of the basic themes of Islam is that one must not take anything for granted; one's hearing, one's sight, one's speech are things for which one must be profoundly thankful, whereas these things man has come to take for granted. And this is one aspect of the primordiality of Islam. As the last religion, Islam claims to be the primordial religion, and this wonderment recalls the wonderment of the first men who were created on Earth and who took nothing for granted, and who saw the marvels of creation and marvelled at them spontaneously. That is another of the messages of the Qur'ān.

Now, I think that I have probably said enough. There may be questions that some of you want to ask, but I will just end with a quotation about the Qur'ān from what is probably the best general book ever written—at any rate this century—about Islam, which is called *Understanding Islam*. It is by Frithjof Schuon:

> ... the verses of the Qur'ān... are not only utterances which transmit thoughts; they are also, in a sense, beings, powers, talismans. The soul of the Muslim is as it were woven out of sacred formulae; in these he works, in these he rests, in these he lives, in these he dies.[21]

That is something which must be understood if one is to

[21] Frithjof Schuon, *Understanding Islam*, first published in English in 1963. The wording of the quotation may come from the original French.

understand Islam: the tremendous importance of the Qur'ānic verses, of which it is no exaggeration to say that the soul of the Muslim is woven.

The Universality of the Qur'ān

LADIES AND GENTLEMEN, I was intending to begin my talk with a quotation from Frithjof Schuon which seems to me to be very relevant to the present time, and also it is relevant to this talk, because he points out in a very clear way that the fact that so many people no longer practise religion, and others no longer believe in religion, it is not altogether the fault of modernism; the representatives of religion have also to bear a certain responsibility for this, because they have not realised that their usual arguments have become rather outworn. I just repeat exactly what he says:

> The usual religious arguments, through not probing sufficiently to the depth of things, are psychologically somewhat outworn. If human societies degenerate on the one hand with the passage of time, they accumulate on the other hand experiences in virtue of old age, however intermingled with errors these may be, and this paradox is something that any religious teaching should take into account, not by drawing new directives from the general error, but on the contrary by using arguments of a higher order, intellectual rather than sentimental.[1]

And that is something which he does in his books very much. He uses arguments of a higher order, that is, intellectual rather than sentimental, and let us therefore apply these words. One might say one aspect of the wisdom of old age is a calm

---

1 From the chapter "The Human Margin" in *Form and Substance in the Religions*.

objectivity, and let us apply these words to ourselves at the present moment. Here we are in this hall, you to listen and then perhaps to ask questions, I to speak, and our subject is the universality of the Qur'ān.

In the relatively near past this subject might have been considered dangerous, and avoided for fear of causing outbursts of anger; but it is now, I hope, a possibility, because everyone in this room is now in his or her old age. Even the teenagers, if there are any here, because we belong to a society that is old and experienced, and we are therefore faced with the choice offered us by old age between wisdom and senility—these are the two possibilities offered us by old age. Unfortunately, the vast majority of people have already chosen the latter without realising it, but, nonetheless, there are some who welcome what characterises old age, which is calm objectivity.

One of the passages where the Qur'ān is exceedingly universal is this—and in this passage God is not only addressing Muslims, this passage of the Qur'ān is addressed collectively to all members of all the religions in the world—and I will read you just a translation of this passage: *To each of you We have established a law and a way, and if God had wished He would have made you one people; but*—and then we have to understand the words—*He hath willed it otherwise that he may put you to a fair test in what He has given you.*[2] That requires a comment, but the comment is fairly easy to understand, that the idea is that if God had given only one religion to the whole world, it would not have been a fair test, because that religion would have been more suited to some people than to others. So to each people He has given what their particular nature required. The different communities of the world do differ very considerably one from another, and He did this, I repeat: *that He may put you to a fair test in what He has given you. So vie with one another in good works: unto God ye will be brought back, and He will inform you about that wherein ye differed.* He promises to explain, when we

[2] 5:48

come before Him after time has finished, the differences; we will come to understand the differences between the different religions.

Then there is another passage in the Qur'ān which says: *For every people there is a messenger*, that is, a bearer of religion, *some of them We have mentioned, others We have not mentioned.*[3] That, for example, should enable all Muslims to see that Buddhism is a divinely sent religion, because if we look at the world as it is today, there are only three world religions. There are other religions, of course: Hinduism, which is for one people alone, and Judaism is another religion which is only for one people; but if we look at the world as it is, we see, roughly speaking, that God has given the West to Christ, the East to the Buddha, and we are a middle people, as the Qur'ān says: *You are a middle people*,[4] that is, we are between the East and the West, and it is not possible not to accept Buddhism as one of these religions, because the Buddha founded a world religion in the East which has lasted for over two thousand years, and only a *rasūl*, that is, a divine Messenger, could do that. If it had been a false religion, it would have disappeared almost immediately— false religions have come and gone, of course— but Buddhism has to be accepted.

There are many other expressions of universality, and what I propose to do during this talk is to take some of the problems which appear to be contradictions between the different religions, and things which one religion seems to believe and another cannot accept and so on, just to take one or two examples to show that what I have quoted from the Qur'ān is maintained by God throughout.

I thought I would mention just out of general interest, again speaking of the late Frithjof Schuon, that he insisted that it was not conceivable that Christ, in speaking of the future, should not have mentioned, and I quote here his words: "the one unique and incomparable apparition which was to take

[3] 40:78 [4] 2:143

place between His two comings"—between the first and the second coming of Christ. This "one unique and incomparable apparition" is the coming of the Prophet Muhammad. There is nothing else between the first coming of Christ and His second coming but that. He could not have failed to mention this. There is a very clear reference to the Qur'ān and the Prophet in the Gospel of Saint John; it is chapter 16, from verse 12, but the extraordinary thing is that it has never been understood by Christians as a reference to Islam. I will just read the passage to you and you will see. This is towards the end of Christ's first coming: *I have yet many things to say unto you, but ye cannot bear them now. Howbeit when he, the spirit of truth, is come, he shall guide you into all the truth: for he shall not speak from himself; but whatsoever he shall hear, these shall he speak: and he shall declare unto you the things that are to come. And he will glorify me.*[5]

That is clearly a reference to the revelation of the Qur'ān, but it is not mentioned by Muslims or by Christians ever in that way, and I have never heard a Muslim claim that that is a reference to Islam, although there are other passages which are mentioned by Muslims sometimes. *When he, the spirit of truth is come, he shall guide you into all the truth: for he shall not speak from himself; but whatsoever he shall hear, these shall he speak.* But *he shall not speak of himself*—of course, the Prophet did speak of himself too, but his main message is the Qur'ān, which he was made to hear: *but whatsoever he shall hear, these shall he speak.* That is clearly a reference to the revelation of the Qur'ān, but people are not very patient, and it never occurred to Christians; they would have had to wait six hundred years before this took place, and it never occurred to a Christian that the second coming of Christ would not be fairly soon, so this passage is usually interpreted by Christians as referring to the miracle of Pentecost, when the tongues of flame descended and people were able to speak languages which they did not know. So it has never been applied to the

[5] St John 16:12–14.

coming of Muhammad, but nonetheless it remains there, and it is significant also in other ways: the Prophet is called *the spirit of truth*, and this is also very significant as regards the difference between religions. Of course, there must always be truth in every religion, and there must always be love—love and truth, but one of the two is likely to predominate because of the needs of different peoples.

To give an example that explains also why it is not possible really for God to give just one religion to the whole world—because different peoples do have different needs—let us consider the difference between Christianity and Islam, which is very great in so many ways. Christianity is a religion in which, one might say, love predominates over truth. Nobody is implying that there is any falsehood in Christianity, but it is a question of what has the most effect. Let us consider one aspect of Christianity: it is a rather dramatic religion, and in the Christian calendar throughout the year there are the great days; there is the birth of Jesus at Christmas from a virgin mother, and there is the even greater day of the Crucifixion and the Resurrection—and I will come back to the Crucifixion later, because it is another point where there seems to be a difference between the religions. And let us try to imagine in the Middle Ages the beginning of sacred drama with the miracle plays, which played quite a large part in mediaeval Christianity, the beginning of which was something very simple.

On the morning of Easter Sunday, the people of the community scattered over the country would gather together. For example, imagine in England there would be different communities and there might only be one church, and those who went just to the same church would gather together in an open place and this very simple drama would take place; and the drama was this: the coming of the three apostles of Jesus to the cave where they had buried his body with a big stone in front of the cave to prevent the Jews from taking away the body during the night; the Friday was the day of the Crucifixion—what the Christians call Good Friday—and on the Sunday morning, the three of the apostles of Jesus came to the cave with the stone across it to look at the body; and instead they found that this very big stone had been rolled away from the mouth of the cave, and an angel was standing there, and the play is this quite simply: the angel says to the three men: "Whom do ye seek in the sepulchre?" *Quem quaeritis in sepulchro?*—of course, this would have been played in Latin—and the three men reply: *Jesum Christum Dominum Nostrum*, "Jesus Christ our Lord." The angel replies: "He is not here," *Non est hic; surrexit*, "He has risen from the dead."[6] And at that moment the whole congregation of people would be in floods of tears—tears of thanksgiving. But what could be less Islamic than such an occasion? It shows us how they needed a different religion which would suit them, and it worked wonderfully during the Middle Ages. But then, with time there was a degeneration of the religion; and this happens also with us, and as we know, in Islam things are going from bad to worse in general, but in Christianity the religion became over-sentimental, people's intelligence was set free for other things, and the result is the modern civilisation which began, after all, in the Christian West, and has now spread all over the world.

But to go back to the Qur'ān, let me quote one or two expressions of universalism: *Verily, those who believe*, that is, the Muslims, *and those who are Jews, and Sabeans*—it is not certain what people "the Sabeans" refers to, and it is given different interpretations by different commentators—*and Christians: whosoever believeth in God and the last day, and doeth good, no fear shall come upon them, neither shall they grieve.*[7] Now, many Muslims are largely ignorant of the Qur'ān; they live on one or two verses which they have to use in the

[6] Other slightly different versions are found in John Gassner (ed.), *Medieval and Tudor Drama*, Applause: New York and London, 1987.

[7] 5:69, and with variations at 2:62 and 22:17.

prayer. Also, some of the verses of the Qur'ān have been abrogated, and the verse I just quoted is one of those of which people have said: "This verse has been abrogated by other verses." But there is an old Muslim commentary on the Qur'ān in the Middle Ages about this particular verse I read, and one commentator says: "This verse can never be abrogated, because it contains a promise from God, and God does not break His promises"—a wonderful commentary, but that has not stopped other later commentators, many of whom have declared this verse to be abrogated by other verses.

One of these verses which is very popular with such people is the following verse in the Qur'ān: *He it is who has sent His messenger with guidance and the religion of truth, that he may make it prevail over all religion, though the idolaters be averse.*[8] And they also like to interpret the words of a verse: *and verily religion with God is* islām,[9] which occurs in the Qur'ān. But if we take the Qur'ān as a whole, it is quite clear that the word *islām* must be used in this verse in its literal sense, meaning "submission to the will of God," which characterises every religion; there can never be a religion without *islām*, in the sense of submission to the will of God; that is something which characterises all religion. And as to the previous verse that I read: *He it is who has sent His messenger with guidance and the religion of truth, that he may make it prevail over all religion, though the idolaters be averse*, we have to add, there are two ways of interpreting that verse: either we have to add the words "once again": *He it is who has* "once again" *sent His messenger with guidance and the religion of truth, that he may make it prevail over all religion*, because when did God send a religion of untruth? –one has to put in the words "once again." After all, people who take this as meaning that Islam has wiped out all other religions, as many people like to do, they forget that *Sayyidna 'Īsā*, that is, Jesus, was sent with the religion of truth to the Greeks and Romans that He may make it prevail, although the idolaters be averse. Jesus

[8] 9:33 [9] 3:19

had to deal with gods and goddesses of the ancient world, and it took him longer to make Christianity prevail than the Prophet of Islam was able to do with great speed, thanks to—well, thanks to God, of course. Or one can take this particular verse simply to refer to the difficulties had by Muhammad in Arabia: *He it is who has sent His messenger with guidance and the religion of truth, that he may make it prevail over all religion*, that is, what was left of idolatry in Arabia, because the Arabs in the time of the Prophet, except for very few, were all idolaters. That verse can be taken in that limited sense, and the Prophet was able, with the help of God, to make his message prevail over all religion that was in Arabia.

Let us take one or two other examples of universalism; there are many arguments which can be used. If we take the case of England, for example, England was converted to Christianity in the lifetime of the Prophet Muhammad. It would have been quite easy, if God had wished, for Him to have spread Islam across France from Spain, but there was a point in Spain where the Muslims knew that they could go no further; they were stopped at a certain point. And let me read this other passage now, spoken to the Prophet Muhammad: *And to thee We have revealed the scripture with the truth, confirming what was before it, and a watcher over it.*[10] Now, that is a remarkable thing: a quality of Islam is to protect other religions and to watch over them; and one of the chapters of the Qur'ān is named *Al-Mā'ida*, that is "The Table"; it is sometimes translated "The Banquet," but it takes its name from the Last Supper, which was to be the very heart of the Christian religion, and in this passage I have referred to, the word in Arabic is the word *muhaymin*, a protecting, confirming what was before it and protecting it.

Now, regarding this passage on the Eucharist, the Last Supper of Jesus, first of all let me say, as is known, that in later Christianity, and after the so-called Reformation and so

[10] 5:48

on, there has always been a talk about the bread and the wine: "Does transubstantiation really take place? does it not always remain bread and wine? or, is it really the body and blood of Jesus?" However, the Qur'ān describes the Last Supper in its own way, and what the Qur'ān says is that the apostles of Jesus said to him: *Can God send down from heaven a banquet, which will be for the first and the last of us a sign from Him and a grace?*[11] and having rebuked them for putting such a question that way: "Can God do this?"—of course, God can do anything of the kind that He wants—then Jesus himself prays to God to send down a banquet from Heaven which will be a sign "for the first of us and the last of us." And the question of whether there is transubstantiation or not is completely overcome in that passage, because what was sent down, the bread and the wine, as Christ said himself, was heavenly. It was not earthly food, and it has remained a reality for "the first and the last of us," as in to this day that banquet is still a reality. This answers the question of: "Is it really bread and wine or not?" by the Qur'ān stating that the food at this Christian rite is from Heaven directly; it is not of this world, quite simply. And that is an example of the Qur'ān watching over and protecting other religions.

But now, just to mention this in passing, there have always been men and women in every religion who see that a universal perspective is the only standpoint that makes sense. What I was taught as a child, as an Anglican, amounted to saying that, having kept the whole world in darkness for thousands of years, God decided to send a religion, which He did to one people only, the Jews, and then that was spread in the time of Jesus. One wonders—it just does not make sense at all. But early Christians were troubled about men like Socrates and Plato, for example; what about them? because they were not Christians, they were before Christianity; and Saint Justin Martyr found the solution for that: it became a doctrine of

---

[11] 5:112

Christianity that the Crucifixion is an earthly event which can be dated, but the Redemption of people transcends this world, and is therefore beyond time and space. So the Redemption, which according to Christianity coincides with the Crucifixion, is not to be dated; it works backwards to the time even of Adam and Eve.

But as to the Crucifixion itself, this seems to be a contradiction between the two religions, and it raises a problem, because there has never been a Christian who did not believe in the Crucifixion. The average Muslim denies the Crucifixion, and points to a verse in the Qur'ān which we will consider, but there has never been a Christian who did not believe in the Crucifixion, and is it possible that God could base a religion on a lie? It is clearly not possible. But if we examine the words of the Qur'ān, we see that the truth is different from what I have just mentioned. The passage in the Qur'ān is this: *The Jews say, "We have killed the messiah, Jesus, the son of Mary, the messenger of God,"*[12] and the Qur'ān quotes this, one sees: *The Jews say*—they claim—*"We have killed the messiah, Jesus, the son of Mary, the messenger of God."* One might say it is a typical example of Jewish sarcasm. The Qur'ān goes on to say: *They killed him not, nor crucified him, but it seemed to them that they had done so.*[13] Now, the Muslim argument, that the Crucifixion did not take place comes from that, but there are other things to be considered. When the Prophet was asked on one occasion: "When did you become a prophet?" his answer was: "I was a prophet when Adam was between water and clay,"[14] meaning that prophethood is beyond time—it is not subject to earthly time; and the Jewish claim to have killed the Messiah Jesus, the Messenger of God, is a false claim, because they could not kill his prophetic nature—it is beyond time.

The fact that Jesus has two natures is an important point

[12] 4:157 [13] Ibid.

[14] With the variation "... between the spirit and the body", this hadith is found in Tirmidhī.

of Christian doctrine—a human nature and a divine nature. It was the human nature that they killed, and that was crucified. "But it seemed to the Jews that they had done so," and that explains the difference between the Muslim denial of the Crucifixion and the fact that it is the very basis of the Christian religion, because as I say, there has never been a Christian that did not believe in the Crucifixion, and the sign of the Cross is something which characterises the whole Christian religion. But from the Muslim point of view, we could say also, apart from the explanation that I have just given, that one cannot crucify a Messenger of God, and the words of the Qur'ān denying the Crucifixion clearly refer to the denial of the Jewish claim that they have killed the Messiah, the son of Mary, the Messenger of God. One cannot kill a Messenger of God, although it seemed to them that they had done so.

But it could also be said from an Islamic point of view, if one takes the word "crucifying" meaning "putting to death," that if a man is put on the cross one day and two days later is in perfect health, it can be said that he has not been crucified, and that is what is the case there. But the false claim of the Jews was to have killed the spiritual nature of Christ, which is not a possibility. That is how the Qur'ān has to be interpreted in this particular case.

In this particular connection of universalism, one has to understand that there are different degrees, different points of view, different levels of reality which have to be taken into consideration. For example, there is a Christian saying: *None cometh to the Father but through me*,[15] which Christians live on, and which seems to justify them in their lack of universality; but the Prophet of Islam said more or less the same thing about himself, and there is no contradiction, because clearly this was spoken by both the prophets in question from the point of view of the *Logos*. A divine Messenger, *rasūl*, is the *Logos* in human form, and this saying of the Prophet was

[15] St John 14:6.

clearly from the point of view of the *Logos*, so it is possible for every *rasūl* to say: "No one can come to God except through me." And that is not a lack of universalism; it is a truth at that level, if the words are uttered from the level of the *Logos* itself.

The Qur'ānic Doctrine of the Afterlife

BEFORE I BEGIN, I SHOULD perhaps remind you that the Qur'ān is not a book written by man. It is a divine Revelation, and it combines many aspects and many purposes, and it does not express anything like a particular doctrine of something or other. These are flashes of light which we find throughout the Qur'ān, and many of them—most of them, in fact—need commentary, need drawing together and comparing with other flashes of light that relate to the same thing. You will understand what I mean by this better as we go on.

The Qur'ān makes it clear that there are many degrees in the hierarchy of the Hereafter. But let us begin by considering the most decisive division, which draws a line, as it were, between those who are saved and those who are not saved. To these two categories evidently correspond the two main divisions of the Hereafter, namely Heaven or Paradise, and Hell.

What is it that qualifies man for salvation? The answer is given by the Qur'ān immediately after the account of the Fall, and I quote from the Qur'ān: *Then Adam received words from his Lord, for He [God] relented unto him; verily He is the Ever-relenting, the All-merciful.... There shall come unto you from Me a guidance, and whoso followeth My guidance, no harm shall come upon them, neither shall they grieve.*[1] Notice here that this is the plural: *There shall come unto you from Me*; He is speaking here

[1] 2:37–38

not only to Adam, but to his descendants. Thus we see that the condition for salvation is following a guidance from God, that is, a religion revealed by God. Other verses show that the religion must be followed in full, but implicit in His Names *the Ever-relenting* and *the Ever-forgiving*, there is an allowance made for difficulties, especially in hard times. There is a saying of the Prophet: *Verily ye are in an age wherein if ye neglect one tenth of what is ordered ye shall perish; but hereafter a time will come when he who observeth one tenth of what is now ordered shall be saved.*[2] The somewhat negative definition of salvation as escape from all harm and grief has a very positive ring in the Arabic, and it is complemented by the many Qur'ānic descriptions of Paradise—the joys of Paradise—into which the saved are ushered by the Angels. All that they desire is given them there in lasting perfection.

The Paradises are inevitably told of in the Qur'ān in terms of earthly joys. Non-Muslims have made this a point of criticism against the religion, to say that the conception of Paradise is very materialistic. But that is a way of putting things quite the wrong way round. There is a holy tradition[3]—that is, a tradition in which God speaks Himself on the tongue of the Prophet: *I was a hidden treasure and I loved to be known, and so I created the world.*[4] For "world" we could understand "universe," and this means that the earthly state shares with the rest of creation the privilege of being a mirror in which God manifests Himself. Moreover, it is the only mirror accessible to us in this life, so there is a constant refrain in the Qur'ān that we should meditate on the wonders of this world as Signs of God.

This world is precious inasmuch as it serves to manifest or reflect the Hidden Treasure; but it is vanity inasmuch as it is no more than a reflection, and because it is of all reflections the faintest and most remote. The Paradises are incomparably

---

2 Recorded by Tirmidhī. 3 *Ḥadīth qudsī* in Arabic.

4 There is no known *isnād* (chain of transmission) for this hadith, although it has been widely used by Sufi authorities over the centuries.

nearer to the Treasure Itself. They are in fact what they are through being in the very aura of the Treasure, which is mirrored in them with incomparably greater clarity. And so another constant refrain of the Qur'ān is the vanity of this life, its mediocrity, its frustrations, its brevity. For example, this verse: *This lower life is naught but a pastime and a game; and verily the abode of the hereafter, that, that is life, did they but know.*[5] Both these refrains—the negative and the positive—about this world are a basis for the Qur'ān's descriptions of Paradise: on the one hand, the incomparable superiority of the Hereafter is affirmed as in the verse just quoted, or as in the following verse: *No soul knoweth what is secretly stored up for them of coolness of the eyes in reward for what they were wont to do.*[6]

"Coolness of the eyes" is an Arabic expression which means joy or delight. But if the joys of Paradise are unimaginable, they are not totally so, because the joys of this life are there to give us an inkling of what to expect and what to hope for. Let me quote another passage: *Give good tidings unto those who believe and who do deeds of piety, that verily they shall have gardens of paradise watered by flowing rivers. Whenever they are given to eat of one of the fruits thereof, they say, "This is that which we were given aforetime," and they were given a likeness of it.*[7] That means that the fruits of Paradise are like archetypes for the fruits which we eat in this world. The people of Paradise, when they taste of a paradisal fruit, it faintly reminds them of something they had on Earth, although it was not the same. What they had on Earth was just an image or reflection of what they are now eating.

In a word, the universe is a hierarchy of worlds one above the other, all reflections, growing fainter and fainter, of the Hidden Treasure which they were created to manifest. There

---

[5] 29:64

[6] 32:17

[7] 2:25

would be no gardens in this world if it were not for the gardens of Paradise, and no rivers if it were not for the rivers of Paradise; and the gardens and rivers of Paradise themselves would vanish if the Hidden Treasure of the Divine Essence were not Itself the Garden of gardens and the River of rivers. And indeed all will vanish when the Treasure reabsorbs into Itself everything that It has manifested.

Another Qur'ānic refrain is: *Do not all things return to God?* and: *Unto God is the ultimate becoming*. There is also the divine Name "the Inheritor," "the Heir"—*al-Wārith*—which contains in Itself the same meaning: it is God who inherits everything from this world and from the next world.

Perfect contentment is stressed in the Qur'ān as an essential characteristic of Paradise, which means that every blessed spirit has all that he or she is capable of desiring; but there is necessarily an immense hierarchy of Paradises to meet the vast difference of personal capacity to receive. The Qur'ān says: *Behold how We have favoured some of them above others*—that means some of the people in this world above others—*and verily the hereafter is greater in degrees and greater in hierarchic precedences*;[8] and the Prophet said, commenting perhaps on this verse: *The people of paradise will behold the high place that is above them, even as they now behold the bright planet on the eastern or western horizon*,[9] referring to the planet Venus, which shows itself as particularly bright.

One might raise the question in this connection: how is it that those in the lower Paradises can be absolutely content when they know that above them are much greater joys for other people? And you will remember that in *The Divine Comedy* Dante asks precisely the same question in one of the Paradises of one of the blessed spirits: "How is it that you are content?"[10] Well, the answer has already been given in the

[8] 17:21

[9] Recorded by Bukhārī and Muslim.

[10] *The Divine Comedy*, "Paradiso", III, 64.

sense that everybody is satisfied in Paradise; he has all that he can desire, but there is also always the possibility of rising to a higher Paradise. But the answer given to Dante is in fact the very essence of Islam, strangely enough. The answer was, in Italian: *E'n la sua volontade è nostra pace*,[11] that is, *In His Will is our Peace*. Nothing could be more Islamic than that.

Yet the disparity of degrees corresponds exactly to the disparity of receptacles, and each receptacle is full in Paradise. Though the Paradises are numberless, it is nonetheless possible to make divisions in the hierarchy, and one sura in the Qur'ān—the chapters in the Qur'ān are called suras—divides mankind into three groups, which amounts to a twofold division of those who are saved; the three groups are: *those on the right*, *those on the left*, and *the foremost*.[12] *Those on the right* are the generality of believers who are saved; *those on the left* are those who are in Hell; *the foremost* are those who have reached the highest sanctity, and it is said of these that there are many in former generations and few in later generations, whereas of *those on the right* it is said, *many in earlier generations and many in later generations*.[13] One of the other differences between the two is that *the foremost* are given wine to drink, and *those on the right* are given water. But the main difference is that the *foremost* are qualified as *Those who are brought near*[14]—*al-muqarrabūn* in Arabic—those who are brought near to God. It is equivalent to what other religions mean when they speak of union with God; equivalent, for example, to the Hindu *yoga*, but in Islam it is not customary to speak of union with God. However, the measure of nearness can be ascertained by the verse in which God says, *We are nearer to him*—man, that is—*than his jugular vein*.[15] That nearness is equivalent to union, and *the foremost* are those who are brought near to God. It is significant that this word is also used to distinguish the

[11] *Ibid*, III, 85. [12] 56:8–10 [13] 56:39–40
[14] 56:10 *et passim*. [15] 50:16

Archangels from the Angels: the Archangels are the Angels which are brought near, *al-malā'ikatu 'l-muqarrabūn*.[16]

So that is two groups in Paradise: the highest of the spirits and the generality. But another sura—in fact, two other suras—make a third distinction of a group which lies between the two: a group called *al-abrār*, which is usually translated as *the righteous*, and the characteristic of these is that they drink draughts which have been flavoured at the two highest Fountains of Paradise.[17] Now, *the foremost*, of whom we have just been speaking, are said to drink at one of these two highest Fountains which is called *Tasnīm*,[18] and is perfumed with musk; but another aspect of these *foremost* is that they are, as it were, extinguished in God. They are called the *slaves of God*, and are represented as drinking at the cold Fountain of Camphor, *Kāfūr*,[19] which is the other of the two supreme Fountains of Paradise. *The righteous* drink sometimes a cup which is flavoured at the Fountain of Camphor and sometimes from a cup which has been flavoured at the Fountain of Musk. The meaning is clearly that they are following in the footsteps of the *foremost*, of *those who are brought near*, that is, of the highest saints; they are, as it were, on the spiritual path in hope of moving towards the highest spiritual level. I will speak more about these questions in my next talk perhaps, which will be on Sufism.

A question which can be asked is this: do those who are saved go straight to Paradise? The Qur'ān says in one verse, *If ye avoid the great sins ye are forbidden, We will wipe out your faults and cause you to enter with a noble entry.*[20] We can translate the phrase as "wipe out" or "bring to nothing," but this means a purification, and purification is in the nature of things; it is easy to understand. And in fact the Qur'ān mentions a fifth category, that is a fourth category of those who are saved: *the men who are on the Heights*; and in fact these men give their name to one of the suras of the Qur'ān, which is named *The*

[16] 4:172 [17] 76:5 [18] 83:27 [19] 76:5 [20] 4:31

Heights. And what the Qur'ān says is: *And on the heights are men, and they see paradise and hell. They call out to the people of paradise, "Peace be on you." They have not entered it yet, though they are eager to enter.*[21] So that shows that there is a group of people who are saved but who nonetheless have to wait before they are allowed to enter Paradise.

It is to be noted also that in Dante's *Divine Comedy* there are people at the top of the Mountain of Purgatory waiting to enter Paradise, so it would seem that the Heights themselves are a motif for something universal in religion. In Buddhism there is a similar waiting place: those who are not yet ready to enter Paradise are enclosed in lotus buds at the edge of Paradise, buds which open gradually as the souls grow to full maturity.

The Qur'ān tells us no more about those waiting on the Heights, but the necessity for this waiting place can be clearly deduced from what is said about Paradise itself, because the Qur'ān makes it abundantly clear that among the greatest joys of the Hereafter is the company of the blessed spirits. To enter Paradise is therefore a tremendous responsibility, because each spirit must be a source of wonderment and delight to the other spirits, therefore each must be ready for that; each must grow to perfection before entering, that is, each must grow to sainthood.

Another very important point to remember about Paradise is this: one sura of the Qur'ān says that each person will have two Paradises. This is not explained, but it is understandable that since man was created as mediator between Heaven and Earth, he has necessarily a dual nature which needs two Paradises to be fully satisfied. He is on the one hand concerned with the multiple things which immediately surround him, and on the other hand, he is concerned with God—we might say, with the Transcendent. The sura of the Qur'ān in question mentions two pairs of Paradises, one pair higher than the

[21] 7:46

other.[22] According to some commentators, the highest of these four Paradises is not a Paradise in the ordinary sense, but is no less than the Hidden Treasure itself, and it is named *Riḍwān*, or the Paradise of the Essence. Below it, the Paradise that goes with it, the second Paradise, is the Paradise of the Spirit. Together these two Paradises constitute the Hereafter of the greatest saints, including the divine Messengers and the Prophets, because this corresponds to the Prophet's own definition of what he was promised, *the meeting with my Lord and paradise.*[23] In this case, the highest of the two Paradises is *the meeting with my Lord* and the lower of the two is *paradise.*

The word *riḍwān* which I used is very difficult to translate; it means God's acceptance of a saint, His taking him to Himself and whelming him in His Presence. It is sometimes translated by *God's good pleasure*, but I prefer to keep the word *riḍwān*, and I will do so throughout this talk, because it means more—the Arabic word has something of the Absolute about it, and it expresses the highest spiritual possibility; and so when speaking of the saints in Islam, it is customary to add "May God give him or her His *riḍwān*"—*raḍiya'Llāhu 'anhu* or *'anhā.*[24] In this connection we may quote also the following Qur'anic verse: *God hath promised the believers, the men and the women, gardens that are watered by flowing rivers, wherein they shall dwell immortal, and* riḍwān *from God is greater; that is the infinite beatitude.*[25]

Let us also quote another verse, which addresses at death one who is destined for the highest state: *O thou soul which art at peace, return unto thy Lord with gladness that is thine in Him and His in thee. Enter thou among My slaves; enter thou My paradise.*[26] Again we have this same duality: here *My paradise* is the Divine Presence itself, the Paradise of the Essence, for it

22 9:72 23 Bukhārī.

24 The words *riḍwān* and *raḍiya* are derived from the same root consonants.

25 9:72 26 89:27–30

is God who is speaking; and the entry among the Slaves refers to the Paradise of the Spirit, because we have seen that the Slaves in the highest sense are those who alone are allowed to drink at the Fountain of Camphor, one of the two highest fountains of Paradise. The Slaves are those who are completely extinguished before God.

I said that the sura of the Qur'ān which mentions the two Paradises for each person mentions four Paradises altogether, and as to the lower pair of Paradises, their relationship is considered to be analogous at a lower degree to the two higher Paradises. Here the higher of these two lower Paradises is concerned with what is often called beatific vision, whereas the lower is concerned with multiple joys on every side.

Also, those who are in Paradise must be thought of in the present as being in Paradise. This may need an explanation, because one may ask, "Well, what about the Day of Judgement, which is not yet come?" But the answer is that they are above time, and for them the whole temporal cycle is finished. They are above time and therefore, as it were, after the Day of Judgement already, and we on Earth have to consider them as there in Paradise. The Qur'ān says more than once, *Count not those who have been slain in the way of God as dead. Nay, they are living; with their Lord they receive sustenance.*[27] And another verse describes how those who are in Paradise look forward to seeing their beloved ones who are still living on Earth.[28]

We have spoken of *those who are on the Right*, that is, the saved: what of *those on the Left*—the damned? Hell may seem to need some explanation, because, on the one hand, the Qur'ānic descriptions of the sufferings of Hell are unsurpassably terrible, yielding nothing in this respect to the Hindu, Buddhist and Christian descriptions of Hell. But on the other hand, the Qur'ān insists that whereas every good deed is rewarded tenfold, each sin is punished only with its

[27] 3:169 [28] 3:170

equivalent.[29] How then is it possible to deserve Hell? But before trying to answer this question, we must first interrogate ourselves. We may think we are capable of assessing sinful acts such as murder or theft, and we hear today not infrequently of crimes so appalling, and so indicative of a horrible state of soul in the person, that we might say no punishment but Hell is bad enough for this, until we remember that Hell is not just for a day or a week, but seemingly endless. We will come back later to this question of duration.

Nonetheless, are we capable of assessing the gravity of sins which are states lived without respite from one year's end to another, like the sins of atheism and, we may add, agnosticism? The Creator says in the Qur'ān: *I did not create jinn and men except that they should worship Me.*[30] What makes man human is that he should reach beyond this world. The man who fails to worship is subhuman, and not merely that, as the Qur'ān points out, but even lower than the animals.[31] In short, man was created as representative of God on Earth, endowed with immense privileges such as no other earthly creature enjoys.

We may note just in passing that the people to whom the Qur'ān was revealed, that is, the pre-Islamic Arabs in Mecca and nearby parts of Arabia, were not unlike the modern West in certain respects; they were arrogant, they were self-satisfied, and they did not believe in the Afterlife. The great difference between them is that they did believe grudgingly in God, but they did not seem to believe that He paid very much attention to this world, and most of them definitely did not believe in the Afterlife. They believed that death would finish them forever. It is a tremendous difference, of course, between that and the vast number of people in the modern West who simply do not believe in God, and who believe that man is better today than he has ever been. But what would the Qur'ān say of them?

---

29 6:160, and also relevant are 27:89 and 28:84. This is an important aspect of how God's justice is encompassed by His mercy.

30 51:56 31 8:55

It says of the people of Arabia at the time of the Revelation of the Qur'ān—in another refrain, even, running through the Qur'ān—that these people are *blind and deaf.*[32]

Nonetheless, the greatest gift that God has given to man is man's power to conceive the Transcendent, and this does not merely begin in the present life. The Qur'ān stresses that at the creation of Adam every human being later to be born into this world was imbued with the knowledge of the Divine Lordship, *Lest you should say on the day of judgement: Of this we were unaware.*[33] In other words, every human being has in the depths of his nature the sense of the Absolute. This sense may be buried under heaps of rubble, but nonetheless it is there, and according to the Qur'ān the sin of sins is turning one's back on the Transcendent in order to give all one's attention to this world, not as the representative of God, but as a parody of God, a would-be independent tyrant out for an unrestrained and undirected exploitation of all resources of the earthly state.

This is the great betrayal of trust on the part of man, and if Hell seems to have a touch of the Absolute, it is because this betrayal is in relation to the Absolute. But Hell is not absolute, and therefore cannot be eternal, for that is the prerogative of the Hidden Treasure alone. It is true that the Qur'ān speaks of the people of Hell as *abiding therein forever*,[34] but this *forever* has to be understood in a relative sense, for there is one very explicit passage in the Qur'ān in which a double limitation is put on the everlastingness of Hell: its inmates are described in another sura as *abiding therein so long as the heavens and the earth endure, except as God wisheth; verily God is ever the doer of what He will.*[35] The first of the two limitations, *so long as the Heavens and the Earth endure,* can be interpreted "until the Creator reabsorbs the Universe back into Himself." As to the second limitation, it clearly refers to the possibility of a divine

[32] 2:18, 2:171, 6:39 and 8:22.

[33] 7:172 [34] 72:23 [35] 11:107

intervention, and this is explained in a well-known saying of the Prophet that after the Judgement, when the wretched are in Hell and the blessed are in Paradise, God will call together the Angels and the Prophets and the believers and bid them intercede for those in Hell, and in consequence of this intercession a multitude of souls are released. It does not say how long after this, but then God orders the release of all those in whom there is any good, so that only those who have no good to their credit are left in Hell. And then comes the time when He says, *The angels have interceded, and the prophets have interceded, and the believers have interceded, and none is left to intercede but the Most Merciful of the Merciful*,[36] this latter being one of the Names of God. And then He will take out of Hell all who are left, and will throw them into the River of Life at the entrance to the Gardens of Paradise.

The passage in the Qur'ān, on which this is a commentary, goes on to describe the blessed in Paradise as *abiding therein so long as the heavens and the earth endure, except as God wisheth*, and apparently, there is just the same double limitation placed on the everlastingness of Paradise as on that of Hell; but it is not so, for as we have seen, Paradise is, as it were, open to the Absolute—as Hell is not—in virtue of the highest Paradise, that is, the Paradise of the Essence which is the Absolute Itself. And so, in the Qur'ān, immediately after what we have just quoted, *so long as the Heavens and the Earth endure, except as God wishes*, there comes the reassuring promise, *A gift that shall not be taken away*.[37] Such is Paradise: a gift that shall not be taken away.

The Prophet's explanation of this passage continues. After the last people have been taken out of Hell, he said: *God will turn to the people of paradise and say, "Are ye content?" And they say, "How should we not be content?" And He will say, "I will give you better than this." And they will say, "What thing, O Lord, is better?"*[38]

As the Qur'ān says: *On the day when We shall roll up the heavens as at the rolling up of a written scroll*.[39] So Paradise is a

36 Recorded by Muslim. 37 11:108 38 Bukhārī. 39 21:104

gift that shall not be taken away, because although, in fact, it is taken away, it is replaced by the incomparably greater felicity of the Supreme Paradise, which is no less than the Infinite and Eternal Beatitude of the Hidden Treasure Itself, from which all creation proceeds, and to which it all returns.

Now, that is all I can say for the moment. Of course, there are many other things which could be said, but that gives you, I think, the main doctrine of the Hereafter which is to be found in the Qur'ān.

There are many details which could have been mentioned. I might just mention one in connection with the two Paradises, which each of the people of Paradise is blessed with. The commentators make certain interpretations about the fruits they are given. Remember that the higher of the two Paradises is always concerned with the Transcendent, concerned with God, whereas the lower of the two is concerned with the person's own particular desires. Also, it is pointed out by one of the commentators that, in the two highest Paradises, the fruit of the Paradise of the Spirit is mentioned as the date, and the fruit of the Paradise of the Essence is the pomegranate. These must be taken, of course, purely symbolically, but he remarks that, in the date, the kernel of the individuality still remains, whereas the pomegranate is pure fruit; it is all entirely to be eaten. And the same is analogously true of the two lower Paradises. In the lowest of the four mentioned, the fruit is not what we normally call a fruit, it is the olive; whereas, in the Paradise above it, the fruit is the fig. There again one sees the kernel of the individuality is in the olive, but the fig is pure fruit, as it were, without a kernel, without individualism in it.

There are many comments on this sura of the Qur'ān, and I have based quite a considerable part of my little book, *The Book of Certainty*,[40] on what the Qur'ān says about the four Paradises, and about the two pairs of Paradises—two for

[40] Abū Bakr Sirāj ad-Dīn, *The Book of Certainty: the Sufi Doctrine of Faith, Vision and Gnosis*, Islamic Texts Society, Cambridge, 1992.

each blessed spirit—and what the commentators say about the different contents of the various Paradises.

The Qur'ānic Origins of Sufism

THIS TALK IS PARTLY A CONTINUATION of my talk last week on the Qur'ānic Doctrine of the Afterlife, but I think it is nonetheless self-sufficient, that is, that those of you who were not here last week will nonetheless understand what I have to say.

What is mysticism? We speak of "second nature"—something becoming second nature to a man or to men; and one could say that non-mysticism has become man's "second nature." But all religions agree that man was created in the image of God and in a state of intimacy with God, that is, with knowledge of the Mysteries, and that this lost state can be regained. And we could answer the question "what is mysticism" by saying that it is everything that lies between the aspiration to regain this state, the lost state, and the actual regaining of it.

Now, Sufism is Islamic mysticism, but it has not always been fully considered in that way by Western scholars, and one of the reasons is this: if you liken different religions to different points on the circumference of a circle, every religion has an inner aspect which may be likened to a radius from the point on the circumference leading to the centre, and the centre is One. It is the Absolute-Infinite, God Himself. The radii are the different mysticisms, and the nearer they approach the centre the nearer they approach each other, so in consequence Sufism has always appeared much nearer to Christians than the outer aspect of Islam. In fact Western people in general have been greatly attracted by some of the outstanding saints of Islam, like Rābi'ah al-'Adawiyyah, Ḥallāj, Rūmī, Muḥyi'd-dīn ibn 'Arabī, and it was suggested from that that Sufism must have come from a Christian influence on Islam, that it could not have come from Islam itself. Other people, to be original, suggested that it might have been a Buddhist influence; others, a Neoplatonic influence.

The Sufi view of its origins as being Islamic many scholars refuse to accept. There is a prejudice about subjectivity, and it was said that Truth needs an objective judgement. Some Western scholars would say, "We are objective, but we cannot take the opinion of the Sufis because they are being subjective about themselves." Others said that Sufis pretend Sufism to be Islamic in order to be accepted as members of the community and not persecuted. But we must be grateful to Massignon, who was unquestionably a great scholar, for breaking away from these general Western opinions and saying: "Contrary to the Pharisaical opinion of many *fuqahā'*," that is, the legal authorities in Islam, very few of whom understand Sufism, and they tend to welcome the idea that it is not Islamic, "Contrary to the... opinion of many *fuqahā'*, an opinion which has been accepted for the last sixty years by many Arabists, I have had to admit, with Margoliouth, that the Qur'ān contains real seeds of mysticism, seeds capable of an autonomous development without being impregnated from any foreign source."[1] This is refreshing, but as we shall see, it is a very considerable understatement.

The Sufis themselves have never doubted for one instant that Sufism began with Islam itself. The 10th century Sufi Fushanjī said in his time: "Today Sufism is a name without a reality; it was once a reality without a name." And the great Hujwīrī, the author of *Kashf al-Maḥjūb*, commenting on this a hundred years later, said: "In the time of the Companions of the Prophet and their immediate successors this name did not exist, but its reality was in everybody. Now the name

[1] *La Passion d'Al-Hallāj*, p. 480.

exists without the reality,"[2] meaning that today, those who call themselves Sufis are not really Sufis; we have lost the reality of Sufism. This is, of course, a grave exaggeration, but nonetheless commendable in the sense that it shows the very high standards which prevailed in those days. Ibn Khaldūn the historian simply says that at first in Islam spirituality—that is, mysticism—was too general to be given a special name, but when worldliness spread and the majority of people sunk below the mystical level, then Islamic mysticism had to be given a special name.

The word *ṣūfī* means "wearer of wool"; *ṣūf* is the Arabic for wool, and there is no doubt that wool was associated with spirituality even back as far as the times of the beginning of Judaism, the times of Moses. The Prophet mentioned that Moses was dressed in wool when God spoke to him on Mount Sinai, and the fact that he took the trouble to mention that is significant. But the word *ṣūfī* has other possible connections: the letters *ṣād*, *fā*, *wāw*, from which it comes, or rather with which it is connected, if you change them around they have other meanings, and you can say that the word *ṣūfī* is the passive of the verb *ṣāfā'*, which, if God is the subject, means: "He chose him for Himself as a friend," and *ṣūfī* means he was chosen as a friend by God, so that it has this secondary meaning which is very significant. But it is mysterious, and that is an advantage; the Sufis needed a mysterious name because mysticism, Sufism in this case, is mysterious. But no more about the meaning of the word.

What I wish to say first of all is that it was highly significant that the Archangel came to the Prophet when he was in a spiritual retreat. And this practice of spiritual retreats was taken from a group of people in Arabia called the *ḥunafā'*, who were the last repositories of the tradition of Abraham in Arabia. They kept alive the Abrahamic tradition throughout the centuries, and they were in the habit of making spiritual

[2] *Kashf al-Maḥjūb*, ch. III.

retreats, and they, almost alone of the Arabs, were believers in one God and total rejecters of the polytheism which prevailed over most of those parts. And it is precisely the Sufis—and the Sufis alone, one might say—who have maintained the practice of spiritual retreats until the present day. Indeed, that is an esoteric practice. It could be said indeed that the Prophet was a mystic, a Sufi in all but name, before he was actually a prophet, which he became in that cave through the Revelation of the Qur'ān.

Now, to consider the descent of the Qur'ān. Let us quote a verse from it: *If We had sent down this Qur'ān upon a mountain, thou wouldst have seen it humbled, split asunder through fear of God. We coin such similitudes for men that they may meditate.*[3] Here the two immediate objects of meditation for men are firstly the tremendous pressure of the divine Word, and secondly, the amazing strength of endurance of him who received it. In this last connection we may quote another verse addressed to the Prophet himself: *Verily of an immense magnitude is thy nature.*[4] Nonetheless, to begin with, the Prophet had a certain dread of receiving a Revelation, and he told his wife to pile garments over him when he slept; but all to no purpose, for one very early Revelation begins: *O thou who art wrapped in thy cloak, arise and warn.*[5] Another very early Revelation begins: *O thou who art enshrouded in thy raiment, keep vigil all the night save a little; a half of it, or take from that a little, or add to it, and recite the Qur'ān with exact recital,*[6] and then it adds, *And invoke in remembrance the Name of thy Lord, and devote thyself unto Him with an utter devotion.*[7]

We have here, right at the beginning of Islam, the inauguration of what has been throughout the centuries, and still is, the very essence of Sufi practice, the invocation of the Divine Name, with respect to which—that is with respect to this invocation—another early Revelation, having mentioned

[3] 59:21 [4] 68:4 [5] 74:1–2
[6] 73:1–4 [7] 73:8

the power of the canonical prayer, adds: *the invocation of Allāh is greater.*[8] Finally, this particular Revelation, which begins: *O thou who art enshrouded in thy raiment*, it ends with the words: *Verily this is a reminder, so let him who will take unto his Lord a way.*[9]

Another very early sura—that is the name given to chapters in the Qur'ān, so I will speak of suras throughout this talk, and you will understand by that "chapter"—another very early sura repeats these words: *Let him who will take unto his Lord a way*,[10] and mysticism, in this case Sufism, is precisely the way to God, the way beyond salvation to sanctification, which itself is being in God's presence.

It must be remembered that every Revelation received by the Prophet was passed on immediately to his followers, who learnt it by heart and recited it again and again, together with what they had already been given of the Qur'ān. Nor were the verses addressed to him in particular considered as being for him alone, except what especially concerned his function as prophet. Such words as *Keep vigil all the night, save a little*, as also from an already mentioned early sura the words *Glorify Him the livelong night*,[11] these words were taken as being for every member of that first small community in Mecca. And we may note that the first two men to start that community, the Prophet's cousin and future son-in-law 'Alī, and the Prophet's best friend and future father-in-law Abu Bakr, have always been looked back to by the Sufis as the first great prototypes of Sufism after the Prophet himself.

In a word, when we read these earliest Revelations, we are conscious of an élite whose lives were utterly dedicated to God, and whose intensity of worship clearly went far beyond the possibility of all but a few. The path of Islam was at its outset the highly rigorous path of doing one's utmost, unalleviated as yet by the establishment of a legal minimum. We recall in this connection the already quoted saying: "Sufism was once a reality without a name." It had, in fact, a name: *islām*. Nor

[8] 29:45 [9] 73:19 [10] 76:29 [11] 76:26

is it possible to refute the Sufi claim that Sufism is the heart of Islam, a claim admitted throughout the centuries by many non-Sufi Muslims. And I may just point out in this context that it is the Sufis who are, in the strict meaning of words, the fundamentalists. One speaks of Islamic fundamentalists today meaning something totally different from Sufism, but if words are to have their correct meaning, and one is asked who are the fundamentalists of Islam, the answer is the Sufis.

Yet by the end of the Prophet's life, this initial group had become a relatively small minority, and the Prophet received a Revelation which he was told to add to the end of one of these very early suras about which we have been talking: *Verily thy Lord knoweth that thou keepest vigilant nearly two thirds of the night, or its half, or a third; thou and a group of those who are with thee.*[12] It goes on to make the demands less exacting, because of the great number of the people in Islam for whom the Qur'ān was addressed; the Qur'ān was addressed to all Muslims, and these demands were beyond their possibilities. But in virtue of this verse, the Sufis often refer to themselves as "the group"—it is mentioned in this verse, *al-ṭā'ifah* in Arabic. The early Revelations of the Qur'ān predict the minority status of mystics.

As we saw last week in the talk on the Afterlife, in one sura we saw the faithful are divided into two groups, *the foremost* and *those on the right*, that is, the highest saints and the generality. And the *foremost* are said to be many among the first, that is, the peoples of old, and few among the last, that is, the later peoples. And other early suras introduce a third group between the two, *the righteous*, who are clearly those who are following the highest saints, clearly because they are said to be drinking draughts which have been flavoured from the two highest Fountains of Paradise, *Kafūr* and *Tasnīm*, and only the highest saints can approach these fountains or drink from them.

[12] 73:20

These passages relate directly to the theme of this talk, that is, the Qur'ānic origin of Sufism. They relate to it in a twofold way. Firstly, they show that the concept of a mystic élite was altogether familiar to the first generation of Islam. Secondly, they have proved, and still do so, to be an origin of Sufism for members of each new generation. Since it is said of *the foremost* that they are brought near to God, more spiritually sensitive readers of the Qur'ān inevitably ask their elders, "What must I do to be *near*?" or "How can I become one of *the righteous*?" And there is only one answer to that question, though, needless to say, it is not always given.

These suras bring us to another aspect of the mystic content of the Qur'ān. The highest saints are referred to in one passage as *the slaves of God*,[13] yet it is important to understand that certain words are to be understood at different levels. In one sense every creature is a slave of God; even Satan. But in one verse Satan is told, *Over my slaves thou hast no power*.[14] And here the word is clearly used in its highest sense, to indicate those who have realised the fullness of humility and effacement towards God. Ritually it is the prostration in the prayer which may be said to enact slavehood in its highest sense; and the Prophet was told, *Prostrate yourself and draw nigh*[15] in one verse of the Qur'ān, which he commented on by saying, *The slave is nearest his Lord when he is prostrate*.[16] This establishes an identity between the *slaves* and the *foremost*—another name for the highest saints—for the *foremost* are characterised by nearness to God; they are *those who are brought near*, which means those who have realised the fact that God is always absolutely near. To quote the Qur'ān: *nearer to him*—that is man—*than his jugular vein*.[17]

The general situation was wonderfully expressed by the Sufi Farīd al-Dīn ʿAṭṭār, the author of *The Conference of the Birds*,

[13] 76:5–6 [14] 15:42 [15] 96:19

[16] Found in Bukhārī, Muslim, Abū Dā'ūd and Al-Nasā'ī.

[17] 50:16

which many of you have heard of, when he said, "God is near to us; we are far from Him." Analogous to slavehood is poverty; all are poor. The Qur'ān says, *O men, ye are the poor, and God is the rich, the Owner of praise.*[18]

Poverty applies to everybody, like slavehood; but spiritual poverty is the realisation of this dependence on God, and the Sufis like to call themselves "the poor"—*fuqarā'* is the word in Arabic. They use this word far more among themselves than they use the word "Sufi," and the singular *faqīr*, in Persian *darwīsh*, is the origin of fakir and dervish in English.

Near to the question of poverty is extinction, which is used in the Qur'ān, and which represents the necessary prelude to the highest state, which one might say is union with God, except that, from the Islamic point of view, the word "union" is avoided. One plus one makes two; it has to be naught plus one which makes one, because the Oneness has to be maintained, and the naught is what extinction means; one has to reduce oneself to nothingness, as it were, in order to enter the Divine Presence.

Many of these words like "poverty," "slavehood" and so on, are used in different degrees. But there are certain things which are said in the Qur'ān which have to be taken in a profound sense. On one occasion the Qur'ān says: *It is not the eyesights that are blind, but blind are the hearts that are in the breasts.*[19] In the whole of the ancient world the heart—and this is not the physical heart, but what corresponds to it in the psychic substance—the heart was considered the centre of the soul. The bodily heart is, as it were, the projection of the centre of the psychic substance which is the gateway to the spirit, and it is that which is meant here by the word "heart." When one speaks of "the eye of the heart" one is referring to this centre of the soul, not the centre of the body, but of which the centre of the body is as an image, hence, *It is not the eyesights that are blind, but blind are the hearts.* The Prophet said in commenting

[18] 35:15 [19] 22:46

on this verse; *For everything there is a polish that taketh away rust, and the polish of the heart is remembrance of God,*[20] or *invocation of God*, for those words *dhikru'Llāh* can be translated in either way. In other words it is the essence of Sufism which is capable of taking rust away from the heart, the rust which prevents the eye of the heart from seeing.

The heart was known to all ancient tradition as the organ of transcendent vision. We know from the Bible—I think it is from Solomon—*I sleep but my heart is awake,*[21] and the Prophet said that his heart was awake like the hearts of the prophets before him. The wake of the heart, of course, means that the eye of the heart is open. But the Qur'ān makes it clear that this prophetic state can be shared in varying degrees by others. Throughout the Qur'ān, almost as a refrain, are the words: *Only they pay attention who have hearts, only they believe, only they see signs who have hearts.*[22] And this is the nearest thing in the Qur'ān, one might say, to the actual mention of the Sufi: one who has a heart.

This brings us to another essential point, and if we consider what Revelation is and what the heart is, it is through the heart that the vertical axis passes—the vertical axis, known sometimes as the Axis of the Universe, or the Tree of the Universe, *Shajarat al-Kawn*—Muḥyī'd-dīn ibn ʿArabī uses that term. It is really the inward Tree of Life, if one likes. It passes through the heart, and as I said, the heart is generally considered as the gateway to the spirit, that is, the gateway to the Beyond, to all the higher spiritual states.

Now, Sufism is concerned with man's first nature, man's primordial nature. All mysticism is concerned with that. And man was, or is, by his primordial nature the mediator between Heaven and Earth. The first preoccupation of mystics is to adopt what we might call a vertical point of view, and reject what has become second nature to man, that is, horizontality and outwardness. *They only know an outward appearance of this*

20 Bukhārī. 21 Song of Solomon 5:2. 22 22:46 among others.

earthly life,[23] the Qur'ān says in one verse, referring to the majority of people. To enter a mystical order means rejecting totally, as far as is possible, that horizontality and that outwardness, and adopting inwardness and verticality, and by that, adopting the divine point of view instead of a human or worldly point of view. The Qur'ān, like every Revelation, is nothing but verticality. If we are on the horizontal for a few moments we are always being snatched back to God. And on the other hand, there is always mention of descent throughout the Qur'ān continually: sending down rain, sending down the Revelation itself, sending down Mercy.[24] The whole book vibrates, one might say, with verticality, so that the Sufi is, as it were, at home in the Qur'ān in the way that other people are not. When one reads it, one is conscious of that again and again.

People have complained that the Qur'ān does not have many stories in it. The reason of that complaint is that, as I said, one is being continually snatched back to God in the middle of a story, then it continues. There is one particular story, where it is as if somebody had made that complaint to God, and He had said by concession; "Well, I will tell you a story," and that is the story of Joseph, which is wonderfully told from beginning to end, but not again without being snatched up to God several times.

And there are the continual cadences in the Qur'ān. The words "Heaven and Earth," *the Heavens and the Earth*, continually echoing in one's soul after reading the Qur'ān: *al-samawāti wa'l-arḍ*,[25] and for a sensitive person this verticality is bound to awaken the inward verticality which he is trying to make natural to him, to regain his first nature, which is vertical, the nature of one who is the mediator between Heaven and Earth.

[23] 30:7 [24] 6:99, 7:57 and many others. [25] 2:33, 2:107 and many others.

There is another question not unconnected with this. This has also to do with the Qur'ān as Revelation, but it has nothing directly to do with the contents of the Qur'ān, but simply with the Revelation itself. Man was made in the image of God as mediator between Heaven and Earth, and according to Islam the nature of Man has not been changed by the Fall; Man is still virtually what he was created to be, but that first nature has been covered for the vast majority over an impenetrable rubble of second nature. Nonetheless, it is there, and what is the most powerful thing that could awaken this first nature in the depths of men's souls? One might say that the answer is the founding of a new religion, or rather, more precisely, the divine intervention which constitutes the founding of a new religion. To use the image of fire, we can say that this first nature of Man which is hidden in the depths of his second nature is inflammability, and an inflammable substance, if it comes close to fire, is liable to burst into flame.

The descent of the Qur'ān, and in fact the whole period of the Prophet's mission, means a descent into this world of incalculable spiritual powers. The Qur'ān itself speaks of this; one of the suras is named after the night in which the Prophet received the Qur'ān from the Archangel, and that night is known in Islam as *Laylat al-Qadr*, the Night of *Qadr*. The word *qadr* is very difficult to translate. The translation is bound to be too weak; "Night of Power," "Night of Worth," one might say, but I prefer to call it *Laylat al-Qadr—layla* meaning "night." This sura begins: *Verily We sent it down in the* laylat al-qadr*: and what will tell thee what the* laylat al-qadr *is? The* laylat al-qadr *is better than a thousand months. The Angels and the Spirit descend therein.*[26]

This descent of the Angels and the Spirit must be considered, because the Archangel Gabriel was continually present throughout the Prophet's mission. It must be extended to the whole of his mission, and this state of divine

[26] 97:1–4

intervention when the earthly state we are in is penetrated by spiritual influences, that must have caused many virtual spiritualities to burst into flame. I use the symbol of fire because the Sun, as you know, is one of the great symbols of the Spirit; it is therefore legitimate. And it is probably for that reason, that is, the exceptional circumstances of the lifetime of the Prophet after the first Revelation of the Qur'an, the latent spirituality in men's souls was bound to awaken, and it is almost certainly for that reason, or partly for that reason, that the Prophet said: *The best of my people are my generation.*[27]

We cannot ignore in this context the Sayings of the Prophet, because many of them, especially those which relate to Sufism, are what are called Holy Traditions, so called because God speaks in the first person on the tongue of the Prophet. Many other Traditions, those in which the Prophet speaks himself in the first person, are comments on verses of the Qur'ān. He is said to comment on what the Qur'ān says about the heart: *My earth is not vast enough to have room for Me, neither is My heaven, but the heart of My believing slave is vast enough to have room for Me.*[28] That is equivalent to one of the most basic sayings of Christ: *The Kingdom Of Heaven is within you.*[29] It tells us within us lies the Infinite.

Another Holy Tradition answers the question about "nearness," which is so much mentioned in the Qur'ān as if somebody had asked that question: "What do I do to be near?" *My slave ceaseth not to seek to draw near to Me with devotions of his free will until I love him, and when I love him I am the hearing with which he hears, the sight with which he sees, the hand with which he smites, the foot on which he walks.*[30] And that is, one might say, again the essence of Sufism.

And the rites of Sufism are based on what the Qur'ān recommends. First of all, what is obligatory to all Muslims: the five prayers, the fast of Ramadan, the giving of alms,

---

[27] Bukhārī. [28] A hadith often quoted by Sufi authorities.
[29] St Luke 17:21. [30] *Al-Nawawī's Forty Ḥadīth*, no. 38.

the pilgrimage if one can. Then come the devotions of free will which I just mentioned in this hadith, and one of the practices of the Sufis is the saying of the rosary. Usually it contains three formulae: the first one asking forgiveness of God, the second one invoking blessings on the Prophet, and the third one testifying to the Oneness and Transcendence of God. But all these formulae are taken from the Qur'ān itself. Another practice is the spiritual retreat, which I have already mentioned, which one might say is pre-Islamic, but which was taken from the Abrahamic tradition and, like the pilgrimage also which was Abrahamic, incorporated into Islam by the Prophet himself. So that it can be said that Sufism has all its origins in the Qur'ān, and that it began, in all but name, with the beginning of Islam itself.

Aspects of Sufism

IT IS NOT GENERALLY KNOWN that, unfortunately, most Muslims today are very ignorant of the Qur'ān and only know certain verses they use, and that there are many others of which they are unaware. The Qur'ān says very clearly: *To every people We have sent a Messenger; some of them We have mentioned, others We have not mentioned.*[1] The word "people" here may mean a whole continent, or it may be a much smaller area; but if we look at the world as it is today, we see immediately what religions have been sent by God: the great religions of the world, the names of which need not be mentioned. We see also the remains of older religions which also clearly came from God, but they had to be replaced by other religions, because what God gives to Man, Man eventually destroys. The religions of India, Greece and Rome were originally sister religions, and they all clearly came from God. Only Hinduism remains today of those three religions. Those of Greece and Rome were eventually corrupted and destroyed by Man, and had to be replaced by other religions, but Hinduism remains and has retained its truth.

There is a passage in the Qur'ān which is not generally known, and some people like to think it has been abrogated, because it does not fit in with the modern Islamic ideas, but nonetheless it is clearly not. It is a later revelation, revealed in Medina towards the end of the Prophet's life, and the Qur'ān here takes the advantage of speaking not only to Muslims, but

1 Sura *Ghāfir* (The Forgiver), 40:78.

to the whole world, as follows: *For each of you We have made a law and traced out a path, and if God had wished, He would have made you one people.*[2] The next part of the verse is a little elliptical: *But We did what We did in order that We might put you to a test in what We have given you*, that is, "If We had given only one religion, it would not have been a fair test, because that religion would have suited some people better than others, so We gave you many religions." As to the differences between religions, the Qur'ān goes on to say: *Vie with each other in good works; unto Him you will be brought back, and He will explain to you the differences between you,*[3] that is, the vast majority of people do not need to worry about the differences between different religions, because God promises that when We return to Him, He will explain to us the differences between Islam, Christianity, Judaism, Hinduism, Buddhism, and so on.

I was once asked an intelligent question by a Muslim lady as to whether I thought that the Buddha was one of these Messengers whom God sent to a people, and is the Buddha one of those who are not mentioned in the Qur'ān? I answered that he was, without a doubt, because the Buddha founded a world religion which has remained for over two thousand years, and which is still alive, and only a Divine Messenger could do that. God would not have allowed any pseudo-prophet to found a world religion like that. What this verse of the Qur'ān tells us can be illustrated by a large circle, where the different religions sent by different Messengers to all the people on earth are represented by points on the circumference. From every point there is a radius moving to the centre, and this centre is God Himself. The answer to the question: "What is Sufism?" is that Sufism is the radius which leads from the point on the circumference which is Islam to the Centre. That is precisely what Sufism is. And as every radius from each point on the circumference approaches the centre, these radii become nearer and nearer to each other.

---

2 Sura *al-Mā'idah* (The Table), 5:48. 3 Ibid.

On the circumference there is some distance between the point where Christianity starts, the point where Islam starts, the point where Hinduism starts, the point where Judaism starts and so on, and each radius represents the inner, or what is sometimes called the mystical aspect—the mysticism in question of each religion. And as the radii approach the centre and become nearer and nearer to each other, every religion in its mysticism is relatively near to the other religions. That is why, in India, Sufis throughout the centuries have lived in harmonious relationship with their Hindu equivalents, and in many parts of India Sufi orders and the corresponding Hindu orders have been in communication with each other. It has even happened in the past that Hindus, when their guru died, have noticed that the Muslim shaykh who is guiding the Sufis in a nearby village is more spiritual than their own guru's successor, and it has been known that they have come to the Sufi shaykh and asked him to be their guide while remaining Hindus, and the Sufi shaykh has agreed to do that. And the opposite has happened, that Sufis have sometimes come under the guidance of a Hindu guru when they felt that he was the most spiritual man they could make contact with.

It is often said that in the beginning Sufism had no name. Ibn Khaldūn, a famous Muslim historian of the Middle Ages, said that at first spirituality was too general to have a special name, but when worldliness spread, then a special name was necessary, and the inner aspect of Islam came to be called Sufism. But already in the tenth century many Sufis felt that Sufism itself was degenerating to a certain extent, and was not the same as it was. In the 10th century a great Sufi said: "Today Sufism is a name without a reality; in the beginning it was a reality without a name."[4] And then Hujwīrī in the eleventh century commented on this, saying that in the time of the Companions of the Prophet the name "Sufism" did not

[4] Abū'l-Ḥasan Fushanjī (d. 348/960).

exist, but the reality was in everybody, but that now—by the eleventh century—the name exists without the reality. That is clearly an exaggeration, but nonetheless, one can say also that in fact there was a name, and that *Islām* was the first name of Sufism. At its beginning Islam was the highly rigorous path of doing one's utmost. It was unalleviated by a legal minimum, and when we read the earliest verses of the Qur'ān, we are conscious of an élite surrounding the Prophet whose lives were utterly dedicated to God, and whose intensity of worship clearly went far beyond the possibility of all but a few, so that when the religion began to spread, the Revelation made the demands less rigorous.

At the beginning, although we do not have exact dates, the Prophet was in Mecca for about twelve years before he went to Medina. But 622 AD is the date of the Hijra, that is, when the Prophet himself went to Medina, and that is the year 1 AH—the Latin *Anno Hegirae*, "the year of the Hijra," which is the first year of Islam. But it was about twelve years before that when the first Revelation of the Qur'ān came in Mecca to the Prophet. In the beginning of Islam there was a certain advantage which has never existed since that time, that is, a total absence of hypocrisy, because there was no advantage, to say the least, in being a Muslim. It was disadvantageous from a worldly point of view, and highly dangerous, so there was nobody who pretended to be a Muslim. But then, twelve or thirteen years later, when the Prophet moved to Medina, and became very quickly the ruler of Medina, there began to be a considerable worldly advantage in being a Muslim. So then the danger of hypocrisy began, and inevitably that has happened more and more since. Spiritual men and women gradually became more and more of a minority, and it is very significant that a very early Meccan Revelation is the sura *al-Muzzammil*, addressing the Prophet and meaning "You who are wrapped up,"[5] because, although he wanted to receive

[5] Sura 73.

Revelations, it was such a tremendous experience that he was frightened. There is a verse of the Qur'ān which tells us: *If We sent down this Qur'ān upon a mountain, it would break in pieces*,[6] and that gives us some idea of what it must have been like for the Prophet, whose soul was much more than a mountain. Nonetheless, it was a very awe-inspiring experience, to say the least, and feeling afraid, he wrapped himself, sometimes telling his wife to put clothes on top of him at night. This particular Revelation[7] begins by telling *Arise* to the Prophet—telling him to arise—and to *keep vigil all the night, save a little*,[8] and this is followed by other rigorous orders; but in the Medina period a final verse was added to this sura, making the demands much less rigorous,[9] because they were bent on doing all that was physically possible, fulfilling the demands of what we know as Sufism—since these first Muslims were clearly Sufis, although without the name "Sufi". They were totally given to God, and they were capable of carrying out instructions such as *Keep vigil all the night, save a little, half of it, or more, or less*, and so on, whereas this final verse which was revealed in Medina says that God does not wish to ask of man too much, and states in effect: "Do what is easy for you"—what you can do with ease, and so forth. Nonetheless, despite that addition of this final verse in the sura *al-Muzzammil*, the Qur'ān continues, throughout its Revelation, to address the small group of Sufis who continue to exist until the present day. And there are many such verses in the Qur'ān which go over the heads, so to speak, of the vast majority of Muslims.

What, for example, is thought by people of the verse: *It is not the eyesights which are blind, but it is the hearts in the breasts which are blind*?[10] The average Muslim, the vast majority of Muslims, they do not know what that means. For them the heart is just the centre of the human body, towards which blood flows, and which keeps the body alive, but in the

[6] Sura *al-Ḥashr*, 59: 21. [7] That is, sura *al-Muzzammil*, 73. [8] 73: 2
[9] 73: 20 [10] Qur'ān, sura *al-Ḥajj* (The Pilgrimage), 22: 46.

Qur'ān, when a verse like this says that it is not the eyesights which are blind, but the hearts in the breasts which are blind, *al-qulūb* (the hearts), is referring to what is called in Sufism "the eye of the heart," *'ayn al-qalb*, that is the centre not of the body, but the centre of the soul. The Prophet himself spoke of being awake like the other prophets before him, that is, that his "eye"—the eye of his heart—is open, and that is something which the average Muslim does not know anything about.

When we read the Qur'ān and we come to the Arabic phrase *akthar al-nās*, "most people"—that is, most Muslims, so called—, we know that something bad is coming. There is no mention of the word "Sufi" in the Qur'ān, since, of course, the name did not exist. The nearest Qur'ānic equivalent to Sufism is the phrase *ūlū 'l-albāb*, "those who have a kernel," which literally speaking is the heart. It is this kernel, *al-qulūb*, which is referred to in this verse: *lā ta'mā al-abṣār wa-lākin ta'mā al-qulūb allatī fī al-ṣudūr*, "It is not the eyesights which are blind, but it is the hearts in the breasts which are blind."[11] The "heart" is the "kernel" referred to by the phrase *ūlū 'l-albāb*.[12] When those words come in the Qur'ān we know that it is going to be followed by something good. And throughout the Revelation of the Qur'ān down to the end, there are many verses which pass over the heads of the majority of Muslims, and which are clearly made for the Sufis themselves.

Now, I will just go on to say a few words about Sufi doctrine. I recounted something in my book on a great Algerian Sufi shaykh who lived at the beginning of the last century, that is, in the 1900s.[13] I never encountered him myself, but I encountered one of his successors, or his successor, and I read that he would say sometimes to some of his disciples:

[11] 22:46

[12] This phrase, in various forms, occurs in sixteen verses, e.g. 2:179, 3:190, 65:10.

[13] *A Sufi Saint of the Twentieth Century*, 3rd ed., Cambridge: Islamic Texts Society, 1993.

"I sometimes wish you had never learnt the words *lā ilāha illā Allāh* (There is no god but God), because you do not understand the meaning." Because the word *Allāh* includes all the Divine Names, *lā ilāha illā Allāh* means also *lā ḥaqqa illā Allāh*: "There is no reality but God." The Sufis say, with regard to their doctrine, they quote the saying of the Prophet: "God was, and there was nothing with him," and they add: "He is now even as He was." They do that with a certain cunning; they know that they are safe from persecution if they express themselves in that way, because the average *faqīh*—that is, a representative of the Islamic doctrine—will not dare to suggest that God changes, that God is subject to change. They say "He is now even as He was," that is, "He *is*, and there is nothing with Him."

The question of union with God does not exist in Sufism, despite the accusations of people about that, because One plus one equals two, whereas One plus naught equals One, and that is the doctrine of Sufism: one must become nothing in order to be with God, and that nothingness is expressed by the word *faqr*, "poverty." That is why Sufis among themselves do not speak of "Sufis," but they speak of the *fuqarā'*, that is, "the poor." "Are all the *fuqarā'* here?" for example, that is, "the poor." Spiritual poverty, *faqr,* in its highest sense means "nothingness." The word *fanā'*, "extinction," is used very much in Sufism to mean the extinction of the individual soul. The soul becomes nothing in order that it may enter the Divine Presence, because only nothing can enter the Divine Presence, and this is what really distinguishes the Sufis from the rest of the community.

Of course, I am not claiming that every Sufi lives up to what Sufism means, and in fact there has necessarily been a degeneration in Sufism, as in other aspects of Islam. But there is another aspect of Sufism that should be mentioned about which I would like to say something before we finish. As you know, the world is made in the image of God. There is a hadith, usually accepted by the Sufis as a hadith *qudsī*—that is, where God speaks in the first person on the tongue of the Prophet, and recognised generally in Islam as expressing a truth: "I was a Hidden Treasure, and I loved to be known, and so I created the world," and sometimes it says: "... and so I created Man," but Man is nonetheless a world in himself; he is the "little world." In Sufi language, *al-kawn al-kabīr* is the "macrocosm"—a Greek word used in English—it is the outer world. The microcosm, *al-kawn al-ṣaghīr*, is the little world of Man. All religions teach that Man was created in the image of God: Judaism, Christianity and Islam, for example, are identical in that doctrine. There is therefore an analogy between Man and God, God and Man made in His image, but sometimes the analogy is inverted. God is, after all, the First of all things, but Man was created the last of all things, on the Sixth Day, after everything else. Another example of inverse analogy is that, in God, the Divine Beauty is more of a secret than the Divine Goodness, whereas in Man, beauty is outward, goodness is inward.

Now, sacred art is only concerned with one thing, that is, the Divine Beauty which is the secret, and therefore sacred art requires as its artists those people who are innermost in the community, who can see inwards more than other people, and those are precisely the Sufis. Now, what are the two great sacred arts of Islam, one might say? What springs first of all to mind is architecture and calligraphy. Those are two of the greatest sacred arts in Islam, and it has been calculated that nearly all the builders of mosques were Sufis, and it has also been calculated that eighty per cent of the great calligraphers, of the great Qur'ān calligraphers who wrote manuscripts of the Qur'ān were Sufis. That is another aspect, and it is the same thing in every other religion. You always have what are called the "mystics," and in Christianity, most of the manuscripts, most of the churches were built by people who were some kind of more or less equivalent to the Sufis. In the Middle

Ages of Christianity, most of the manuscripts, the beautiful manuscripts, were written in the monasteries and the convents. It is the same with other religions, in Buddhism, in Hinduism and in Taoism, in the Far East.

Now, I have not time to say much more, but I would like to read you the end, in English translation, of "The Wine-Song" of Ibn al-Fāriḍ. Ibn al-Fāriḍ lived toward the end of the Middle Ages in Egypt, and he was considered by some people to be the greatest of Arab poets. One of his poems is called *al-Khamriyyah*, "The Wine-Song"; the wine signifies God, or the Divine Presence. Of course, wine is forbidden to Muslims, but things forbidden to Muslims are not all at the same level. We are not promised the meat of pigs in Paradise, which is forbidden; we are promised wine in Paradise, and that is the difference between the two. The "tavern" where the wine is found means the *zawiyya*, that is, the place where the Sufis gather together, because Ibn al-Fāriḍ was a great Sufi. His tomb is outside Cairo, near the eastern desert, and it is considered as one of the seven holiest places to be visited in Egypt. This is how Ibn al-Fāriḍ ends his poem, I will just read you these lines:

> Seek it [the wine] then in the tavern [this is, the wine]; bid it unveil [that is, let the cobwebs be taken off the vessel which holds the wine]
> To strains of music. They offset its worth,
> For wine and care dwelt never in one place,
> Even as woe with music cannot dwell.
> Be drunk one hour with it, and thou shalt see
> Time's whole age as thy slave, at thy command.
> He hath not lived here, who hath sober lived,
> And he who dieth not drunk hath missed the mark.
> With tears then, let him mourn himself, whose life
> Hath passed, and he no share of it hath had.

Keats and Shakespeare

KEATS WAS BORN AT THE END of October—it seems uncertain whether it was the 29th or the 31st of October—in 1795; and he died in February 1821 in his twenty-sixth year. But I am going to speak about simply the two years 1818 and 1819, which were really the two last years of his life, because the whole of 1820 he was in his last illness; he knew that he was dying, and he did not write anything in that year. He died at the beginning of 1821.

It was extraordinary what he went through in those last two years. First of all, in 1818 he spent three months in the spring at his brother Tom's bedside; his brother was dying of consumption, and John Keats himself had the premonition that he himself would probably die of the same thing; he spent the last three months of that year again at his brother's bedside until he died. He had his twenty-third birthday that October while he was with his brother.

There were three brothers, and the other brother George used to say that nobody had understood John so well as Tom, the one who died; they were very close to each other. And then early in the next year it was that he met Fanny Brawne and fell deeply in love with her. It was about that time that he wrote *The Eve of Saint Agnes*, and it is said to have been written on the basis of that love. He wrote also *The Eve of Saint Mark*, and later, in late spring the same year, he wrote the *Ode to a Nightingale*, then later on the *Ode on a Grecian Urn* and the *Ode on Melancholy*, and he began also revising what was to be his epic poem *Hyperion*, the first version of which he was not satisfied with; but in the autumn he broke away from that and he wrote the ode *To Autumn*.

Then three months later he had this fatal haemorrhage, which he knew would be at the end, and he just lived for another year. He described his life during that year as a posthumous life—that extra year—and so one sees in just these two years there was the death of his brother, his love unrequited enough, these wonderful poems which he wrote, and then his final illness.

He did not know, of course, that Tennyson was to say later that century: "Keats would have become one of the very greatest of all poets, had he lived." He also did not know that many critics rank him, on the odes alone, as among English poets second only to Shakespeare. Many critics have said more or less the equivalent of that, not to mention people like Thomas and Bridges, apart from Tennyson. And Keats' own consciousness of his gifts included the sense of a mandate to enrich the world, and in his case, a sense of frustration through increasing premonition of his own imminent death.

After he fell ill for his last illness, he wrote to Fanny, his beloved, saying, "If I should die, said I to myself, I have left no immortal work behind me; nothing to make my friends proud of my memory, but I have loved the principle of beauty in all things. And if I had had time, I would have made myself remembered." He had already made himself more than merely remembered by writing the great odes, but his ambition was to write not them, nor epic poetry, but to write great plays, which, like Shakespeare's, reveal the harmony of the universe; in Keats' own words, "the balance of good and evil."

It is doubtful, to say the least, if Shakespeare would have accepted these words, "the balance of good and evil"; still less would he have accepted another of Keats' formulations of the same, "the love of good and ill," as being the summit of wisdom. But Keats' more mature formulation, "beauty in all things," Shakespeare would no doubt have accepted—subject to correct interpretation, of course.

Now, allow me to say, just by way of parenthesis, to touch briefly on the question of Keats' writing of plays. He was something of a man of the theatre. Of course, one cannot expect anybody to be such a born dramatist as Shakespeare, but Keats was a man of the theatre; he loved attending performances of Shakespeare, and was altogether fascinated by the acting of Edmund Kean, about whom he writes a great deal, and to whom he attributed a real understanding of Shakespeare. Seeing what he writes about Kean's performance of *King Lear*, we would all be very anxious to attend such a performance if it were possible. But as to the plays which are published in volumes of Keats' works, *Otho the Great* is not really Keats' play, and I have never heard of its being acted. I did go through it once as far as I can remember; I did not find it very easy to read, and it did not leave any impression on me, and *King Stephen*, the other play, is just a fragment.

But over a hundred years after Keats' death, some lines were found written in the margin of another unimportant and unfinished poem called *The Cap and Bells*; they had not been noticed before, and they appear to be a piece of dramatic verse which Keats had the idea of writing. They could be spoken as part of a love scene in a play, it seems to me, with great dramatic effect. Probably they were written addressed to his beloved Fanny, but I am sure never sent to her, for that would have been cruel. They were just written in the margin, and he probably forgot about them. But these are the words, and they are, it seems to me, wonderfully suited to drama:

This living hand, now warm and capable
Of earnest grasping, would, if it were cold
And in the icy silence of the tomb,
So haunt thy days and chill thy dreaming nights,
That thou wouldst wish thine own heart dry of blood
So in my veins red life might stream again,

And thou be conscience-calm'd—see, here it is!—
I hold it towards you.

It was just those lines, and that is the end of my parenthesis. I must go on to point out that by nature Keats was endowed not only with amazing poetic gifts, but also with a profound and penetrating intelligence and with dazzling virtues. He was a personification of generosity—I would prefer to say magnanimity, because it is more comprehensive—of resolution, sincerity, and resignation to the Will of Heaven. He is always quoting as though he is fascinated by the words which Edgar in *King Lear* speaks to his father: when his father wants to put an end to his life, Edgar says to him:

... Men must endure
Their going hence, even as their coming hither;
Ripeness is all...[1]

Keats, who loved especially *King Lear*, is always referring to those lines, which, of course, are the equivalent of Hamlet's words, *the readiness is all*[2]—to be ready for death is all.

And when Keats fell in love with Fanny Brawne, being sincerity itself, he fell totally in love, and he expected her to do the same. He wrote to her:

Yourself—your soul—in pity give me all,
Withhold no atom's atom or I die...

Well, she withheld more than an atom's atom. In fact she withheld more than she gave, and he did die; but she was by no means the chief cause of his death, nor, being what she was, could she have given more. But his life might have been prolonged a bit longer if she had given more than she gave. But above all of his gifts—or rather let us say by reason of this combination of excellencies in the way of intelligence, will and virtue—he was a born mystic, that is, in need of the inner or esoteric aspect of religion, the way of sanctification, not merely

[1] *King Lear*, Act V, sc. II. [2] *Hamlet*, Act V, sc. II.

the outer way of salvation, which was all that the religion of his upbringing offered to him.

Keats was raised as a Protestant, and he was probably brought up to be prejudiced against Roman Catholicism, though he was much too intelligent and objective to accept that. But things were going wrong in religion already. As I mentioned in my talk on René Guénon, the fact that at the beginning of this century in France, which is after all a Catholic country—and there were wonderful popes on the throne at that time, compared with what there is now—there was so much prejudice against religion among the French so-called *intelligentsia*, that Guénon decided not to use the word "religion" in his books at all, for fear that they would not be read. He used the word "tradition" instead, and he based his message on what he called "the Hindu tradition."

That was in this century, but things were beginning to go wrong earlier on, and especially in Protestantism, which was much more vulnerable to decay than Roman Catholicism. By being brought up as a Protestant, that meant that Keats had practically no knowledge of Christian doctrine, no knowledge of Christian mysticism, practically no knowledge of the lives of the Saints or the meaning of sacraments, or even the full significance of rites; and being by nature a universalist, he was put off by Christianity's exclusivism, maintaining itself as the only valid religion, and by these years which we are now considering, 1818 to 1819, he had ceased to consider himself a Christian. He accepted Christianity amongst other religions, and he was a believer, but he shrank from speaking about God as others do. For him God was a great mystery, and Keats had come by that time to rely more on his own intelligence than what the Christian religion gave him in the way of information. It was not difficult to think, as many did think at that time, that somehow religion had gone wrong. Keats' friend Leigh Hunt, for example, was always scoffing at religion. Keats himself was groping in the dark intelligently, but not always infallibly.

As to Shakespeare, I have often mentioned that Dover Wilson's having said very rightly that Shakespeare lived in the world of Plato and Saint Augustine. Although it was after the Reformation, the Middle Ages was still, and he was still, as I have always maintained, one of the last outposts of the Middle Ages. Shakespeare was also a born mystic, but in his case, his world—the world of Plato and Saint Augustine—could give him the truths which he needed for his spiritual development. I repeat, that Keats again was also a born mystic, unlike Milton, Wordsworth, Shelley, Tennyson and others, and hence Keats' certitude that Shakespeare—because he saw that about Shakespeare—that Shakespeare was like a beloved elder brother to himself; a totally kindred spirit. Keats wrote in a letter "they are very shallow people who take every thing literally. A Man's life of any worth is a continual allegory—and very few eyes can see the Mystery of his life... Shakespeare led a life of allegory; his works are the comments on it."

The world that Keats was born into had little to give him except what was left of virgin nature. Above all, Shakespeare was his teacher, but he could not ask Shakespeare questions, and despite his great gifts he was groping in the dark without help. Did he know that we are such stuff as dreams are made of, to quote Prospero's words in *The Tempest*: *We are such stuff as dreams are made on.*[3] He might have answered, "The time will come for such truths, but now I am face to face with the world, and must deal with that great problem first."

This man of twenty-four had discovered unaided, except, as he would have insisted, by Shakespeare's help, that this lower world is penetrated by God, and with all his close-knit sincerity he was concentrated on this wonderful truth and bent on conveying it to others. He had sensed directly something of the harmony of this lower universe. But Keats did not yet know, as Shakespeare had well known, that this harmony is not independent of higher harmonies, nor can this harmony

[3] Act IV, sc. I.

in itself be expressed as the balance of good and evil, as Keats had expressed it earlier, with reference to the plays of Shakespeare. The divine penetration of the world necessarily involves the transcending of evil by Good. Even at the end of *Othello*, which does not enter into the Greater Mysteries, nobody could deny that in this harmony, which undoubtedly one feels at the end of the play, evil has been transcended by Good.

Keats needed to have certain things explained to him. He needed to know the difference between good and evil, that is, their totally different substance, nature and origin, because, traditionally speaking, Good comes ultimately from the Absolute. These questions are universal truths to be found in all traditions, and the One Reality is by general agreement recognised. The agreement is not always there, because for Christianity Meister Eckhart had to insist on making a distinction between the personal God and the Absolute Godhead; he insisted on using the word "Godhead," as "Gottheit" in German, to make a distinction between the Divine Essence, the Absolute Reality, and the personal God. He was made by the Church to retract that, but that was just a formality. For Platonists the Absolute is the Sovereign Good, *to agathon*. The Absolute is pure positivity; It is the Sovereign Good. And Saint Augustine and others besides him in all traditions have maintained that it is in the nature of the Good to reveal Itself, to radiate; the Good must radiate. Radiation means eventually distance, which is, one might say, distance from God. Moreover, distance is dangerous, and that—distance—is the origin of evil. And so the two things, good and evil, are of totally different natures: Good springs from the Absolute directly; it is radiation, gradually becoming less and less by distance. But evil simply comes from distance; it is a purely negative thing, it is just distance. Hence the two things in themselves—good and evil—are of different substances, different natures, different origins, and Keats needed to have that explained to him.

He also needed to have it explained to him that Paradise, where there is no evil and no suffering, is in the nature of Man. Paradise was lost at the Fall of Man, but nonetheless Man's primordial nature was not lost. It remained buried under a rubble, one might say, of accumulating second nature, but it is nonetheless there, under that rubble, and Paradise is still Man's true homeland. And that is why children, who in some respects are wiser than their parents, and in one particular respect are unwilling to accept a story which does not end "and they lived happily ever after." That is wisdom on the part of children, not just wishful thinking, and the idea modernists will tell you, that religion is the product of wishful-thinking, is the opposite of the truth. Eternal happiness is what we are made for and what we should aspire to, and what people throughout history—and pre-history as far as one can make out—always have been the world over aspiring to and preparing their way towards.

But in the world as it was in Keats' day, and as it is today, if one imagines that religion has gone wrong, as it certainly has to a certain extent, it is on the contrary not difficult to slip into the error which I have heard people say during my life, it seems to me quite often, when I was young and through every state of my life: "I am not prepared to believe in a God who does not suffer." I have often heard those words, and of course it is totally contrary to the teaching of all religion. The Absolute is pure positivity, but especially in Christianity, the two Natures of Christ play a very essential part in Christian doctrine. Every Christian is bound to recognise that Christ had two natures, and it is only the Earthly nature that suffered. But nonetheless, that Earthly nature is spoken of as God. The Virgin is often spoken of in Christianity as the Mother of God, so that the idea of a suffering God is something one can slip into fairly easily, and Keats had fallen into that very error. And in his poem *Hyperion*, which is about the Titans being overcome by the Olympians, that is, by their children—Saturn, Thea and Hyperion being replaced by Zeus, Hera and Apollo—Keats puts the words of suffering into the mouth of the goddess Moneta (in his second *Hyperion*). It is, as it were, a very compassionate suffering which embraces the whole human race, but which suffers more than any of them. At the end of 1819, when he was revising the poem he suddenly stopped writing it, and I think that he came to realise that this simply is an error. He broke away from it and he wrote one of his most serene and beautiful poems, the ode *To Autumn*—it was the autumn of 1819, and it was in the following spring that he entered in his last illness. He had given himself to his own brother when he was dying, and one of his friends, Joseph Severn, gave himself to Keats after he fell ill. I think for six months he was with him, and he went with him to Italy in 1820; he died in February 1821, and Joseph Severn was with him the whole time.

I will came back to this, but I would like to also mention Keats' *Ode on a Grecian Urn*, which again has an extraordinary and serene beauty. I would just like to read to you a passage from that, because it is also relevant to what we have been speaking of, that is, the penetration of this world by God, this lower universe, and the harmony of the universe. I do not know what particular urn this is; I do not think anyone does know. I will not read the whole poem, but I must say I would rather have these lines than any Grecian urn I have ever seen. And this is a description of one of the stanzas:

> Who are these coming to the sacrifice?
> To what green altar, O mysterious priest,
> Lead'st thou that heifer lowing at the skies
> And all her silken flanks with garlands dressed?
> What little town by river or sea shore,
> Or mountain-built with peaceful citadel,
> Is emptied of its folk, this pious morn?

And, little town, thy streets for evermore
Will silent be; and not a soul to tell
Why thou art desolate can e'er return.

And this is the end of the poem, where he addresses the urn:

When old age shall this generation waste,
Thou shalt remain, in midst of other woe
Than ours, a friend to man, to whom thou sayst
"Beauty is truth, truth beauty,"—that is all
Ye know on earth, and all ye need to know.

By "Truth" Keats clearly means God, and Beauty, of course, is a manifestation of God. This touches on the question of the Divine penetration of this lower universe, this mystery which Keats had discovered, had felt directly, and which he was bent on giving to mankind in plays. It is, of course, a universal doctrine that the divine Qualities do penetrate the world, that is, the transcendent aspect even of this lower world, and the best known example of this is the penetration of divine Justice into this world; from that the Far Eastern religions have the well-known doctrine which is called sometimes in English the doctrine of concordant action and reaction, which means that one can do nothing without there being a reaction to it. It may not come till after death, but one cannot escape from the divine Justice which penetrates the whole of manifestation, and there is bound to be for every action a reaction. This doctrine is especially known in Taoism and, I think, in Buddhism, but it is something which, of course, is really implicit in every religion. One cannot escape from it. It is expressed by Edgar in *King Lear* when speaking to his brother and his father, how they had to undergo what they did through this very law, although he does not, of course, use the words "concordant action and reaction."

But Keats is also telling us that Beauty penetrates this world in the same way; this substance of manifestation is penetrated by the divine Beauty. The late Frithjof Schuon once wrote that whereas in Man beauty is outward and goodness is inward, in God, by inverse analogy, Goodness is outward and Beauty is inward. Beauty ranks among the very deepest and highest Qualities of God, and that is why the sacred arts in all traditional civilisations are always in the hands of the mystics, that is, the people who belong to the esoteric aspect of the religion, as Keats did not in fact, but in potentiality and by his nature. He was conscious of this penetration of this world by Beauty, and that is what he is trying to express in this poem.

I will just read the first and the last stanzas of this poem, which you all know I imagine:

Season of mists and mellow fruitfulness,
Close bosom-friend of the maturing sun;
Conspiring with him how to load and bless
With fruit the vines that round the thatch-eves run;
To bend with apples the moss'd cottage-trees,
And fill all fruit with ripeness to the core;
To swell the gourd, and plump the hazel shells
With a sweet kernel; to set budding more,
And still more, later flowers for the bees,
Until they think warm days will never cease,
For Summer has o'er-brimm'd their clammy cells.

Then, the last stanza:

Where are the songs of Spring? Ay, where are they?
Think not of them, thou hast thy music too,—
While barred clouds bloom the soft-dying day,
And touch the stubble-plains with rosy hue;
Then in a wailful choir the small gnats mourn
Among the riversallows, borne aloft
Or sinking as the light wind lives or dies;
And full-grown lambs loud bleat from hilly bourn;
Hedge-crickets sing; and now with treble soft
The red-breast whistles from a garden-croft;
And gathering swallows twitter in the skies.

Now, just a few words about the end of his life. Keats, as I said, when he entered into his last illness, his friend, Joseph Severn, insisted on keeping him company until the very end. Joseph Severn was himself a devout Christian, and Keats felt within himself the need for a religion, and that was the only religion within reach really, and it had to be made use of, and Severn was just providentially the right person to be with Keats. I am sure I have read somewhere that in his last days Keats asked Severn to read him the Psalms, or some of the Psalms, and one is sure that among those that Severn read would be the Psalm *The Lord is my Shepherd; I shall not want. He maketh me to lie down in green pastures... He restoreth my soul.*[4] I cannot remember where I read that, but what is certain is that Severn read to him during those last weeks extracts from Jeremy Taylor's book *Holy Living and Holy Dying*. I do not think I have ever read this book, and when I was to give this talk I could not get hold of it, as I do not possess it myself, and I would have looked at it in advance. I was unable to do that, I confess, but Jeremy Taylor was born just within Shakespeare's life, and the book is very highly spoken of by many people. He was a Protestant, but verging on Catholicism; he was what we call in English "very High Church," and he got into trouble under Cromwell for that, and was put in prison more than once. He was at one time actually chaplain to Queen Henrietta Maria, and he took the king's side completely, very definitely, in the Civil War, and what I have read about this book has showed that it is just what Keats would have needed, being what he was. He was probably, in fact, more profoundly religious than Severn himself, but unable to practise the religion, which, of course, is of essential importance. But it is, one likes to think, that that possibility was realised at the end for Keats, who was fundamentally profoundly religious in himself.

[4] Psalm 23: 1–3

Well that, I think, is all I can say, or I intend to say, but if there are any questions anyone would like to ask I will try to answer them.

* * *

Q (indistinct): Do you know the phrase "this vale of soul-making"?

A: "This vale of soul-making". I recognise it—it sounds like a phrase of Keats—yes—it must be in a letter; but then I do not think it represents what—that Keats' terminology was chaotic. He certainly used that term "soul-making", and he was—he had the idea that one of the purposes of life was to make one's soul—I do not know what he really meant by that—he speaks in one place that "soul-making" consists of forming one's identity, and he was worried by the fact that he said children do not have time to make souls. It is not a religious idea at all, and not even a true idea; children traditionally can go straight to Paradise, which is all that a man need hope for. Keats was worried that children do not have time for soul-making which, according to Keats, was the accumulation of "divine sparks" which formed one's character, and he felt that evil was necessary in the world to make that as a kind of disciple, to create tensions in one's life. But it is not—this is something that came from his own intelligence, and I do not think it is anything we need to consider profoundly, because it seems to me to be a mistaken idea. And the use of the word "soul" in any case; he practically never uses the word "spirit" as far as I can make out. It is the spirit that the soul comes from, and to which it goes back. At death the soul of a saint is reabsorbed into the spirit. It is only the spirit that can enter Paradise, the blessed spirits that can enter Paradise, but the soul, when on the Day of Resurrection religion represents the soul as rising above—is rising from the ground and being faced with the glorious body of the Resurrection, applies to a body which is risen from the ground which is being reabsorbed into the psychic domain, which itself is being reabsorbed into the spirit. That is what is known as the Glorious Body of the Resurrection, but that only applies to sanctified people, who are on their way direct to Paradise, but I think I have answered your question as well as I can.

Q (indistinct, but referring to *Ode on a Grecian Urn*):

A: No, I do not think he wrote anything; it was written in the summer of the year before—I mean, presumably it was written before the *Ode to Autumn*, but it was written in the summer, that same summer. All these events were crowded into just these two years, it was quite extraordinary, because what Keats wrote before that year was not really anything comparable to what he wrote later, what he wrote in that particular year, and then there was his love, and the death of his brother. In the previous year he spent six months of the year tending his brother, that was in London I think, mostly at any rate—he lived not always in London, he lived in other places near London. He had many friends. Any other questions?

Q (inaudible):

A: Yes, well, there is no problem about that, the spirit belongs to the next world, that is, the hereafter, the world of the heavens and the Paradises. If you consider the hierarchy—it is a good thing—this is something that Keats really needed to have explained to him and it would not have been explained in the religion in which he was brought up: but that first of all—I mean just briefly to define the hierarchy—there is first of all the Absolute Self, which is the sole reality; everything else is such stuff as which dreams are made on; even the Personal God. The Absolute is the sole Reality, the sole Absolute Reality, it is Absolute, Infinite Perfection. That is God in the highest sense. Then there is the personal God, still at the divine level, but at the level of the Christian Trinity and the Hindu trinity Sat-Chit-Ananda, which is the parallel to that—more or less a parallel—but that is not at the Absolute level, but it is nonetheless at the divine level. The comes the Spirit which has a divine aspect and a celestial aspect: the Spirit said the Spirit of God breathed on the face of the waters in Genesis; and you have the same thing in Hindu doctrine: "And the waters were divided." You have in Hindu doctrine the Upper Waters and the Lower Waters; the Upper Waters are what we call the world of the heavens, the world of the paradises, the lower waters are this world. In Islam, in the Qur'ān the same, exactly the same, the two seas, the salt, bitter sea which corresponds to this lower world, and which is what Keats was talking about when he spoke about the harmony of the universe, this lower world, which is also penetrated by the Divine Presence, and the fresh water sea of the next world which is sometimes called the waters of life. And now, the soul, the domain of the spirit rather, the domain of the spirit is the next world. The word "spirit" also has a divine aspect as well as a celestial aspect. In Christianity it is the divine aspect which is stressed, the third person of the Trinity is that divine aspect, the Holy Ghost; in Islam it is the celestial, the created aspect of the Spirit which is stressed, but both religions, I think, at any rate Islam admits the two. I remember once in Egypt—I was living in Egypt—a thing which would not happen in England, I was travelling, going in a tram up to the pyramids, where I lived down the pyramids road, and having collected all the tickets the tram conductor came and sat by me and said, "I want to ask you a question. Is the spirit created or uncreated?" [laughter] I say that sort of thing would not happen in England. And I said both created and uncreated; I explained to him what I have just said now. But then comes the Heart, which is the centre of the soul, but which is nonetheless on the other side of the boundary, it is on the celestial side. It is the *barzakh*, in Arabic, the dividing place between the two seas, between the two waters, sometimes represented by a rock; and the Heart is the entry, the gate of the Spirit, but it is beyond our reach. Mystics in all mysticisms speak of the

"Eye of the Heart." The opening of the Eye of the Heart is the first aim of every kind of mysticism, purification of the soul in order that the Eye of the Heart should open. It is that that Man lost at the Fall, the sight of the Heart; he was cut off from the Heart. Now, it is on the other side of the boundary, on this side of the boundary that I am speaking of, beyond the Heart, that is, lower than the Heart, that the soul begins, the psychic substance begins, and the intelligence which comes straight from the Divine Light becomes human only when it enters the psychic substance. Before that it is pure Spirit. And the word "intellect" was used throughout the Middle Ages to define the faculty, the spiritual faculty, which was concerned with the next world, not with this world, and which was the faculty of the Heart—the throne of the intellect is the Heart in the sense that I have just mentioned, which is again beyond this world, beyond our reach in this world. Then, you might say, the first purely psychic faculty is the mind, or reason. And reason in the Middle Ages was taught—students were taught—that the reason is the handmaid of the Intellect, works under the direction of the Intellect, but it is for this world, it is a worldly faculty. And you could say that the domain between the reason and the Heart, or between the reason and the boundary which would take us to the Heart, if it were open, but which is closed, is the domain of intuition. You can use the word "intuition" as being in that part of the intelligence which lies on this side of the boundary, but above the mind; it still retains some parts of the Intellect, it comes from the Intellect, it is not pure Intellect, but it has certain intellectual aspects which we call "intuition", and that is what the soul and also other faculties, memory, imagination—and the senses are partly psychic and partly bodily—that is where the soul joins onto the body, through the five senses, the senses of hearing, sight, touch, smell and taste, one could say. The order of the senses actually is traditionally hearing, touch, sight, taste, scent. And it is said that when a man is dying, normally speaking, the last faculty he retains is his hearing. When the first to lose is his sense of smell, then his taste, then his sight, then his touch, and finally his hearing. And that is the order and hierarchy of those senses.

Q (indistinct): ... God that doesn't suffer and that it is the personal God that does suffer... a very deep problem, because, as you know,... said God was watching the suffering of mankind, and this was why we have suffering in the world, because God...

A: Yes, but that was a heresy—that was a monstrous heresy, because in fact God radiates, it is a radiation of God which causes in the end evil, by distance, because nonetheless God—you see people used to say—I forget who it was that said this—we are told that God is Goodness itself and All-powerful. How do we explain evil? If God is Goodness itself and All-powerful, He could stop evil. He may be All-powerful without being Good, that would explain it; or He may be Good without being All-powerful; that again would satisfy logic. But that He should be both Good and All-powerful, that means that evil does not exist, but evil does exist. But the answer to that question given by Frithjof Schuon in one of his books that is very convincing and very profound, that the All-power of God—God is All-powerful because He is the Absolute—He is Absolute-Infinite-Perfection—and that All-power is powerful against everything but His nature. That All-power can do nothing against the nature of God. It is All-powerful over everything else but it cannot stop the radiation of Good from God, it cannot stop the Sovereign Good's radiation of Itself, and it is that radiation which produces distance, and it is from distance that evil... there is no evil in, not merely in the Divine, but there is no evil in what one might call the Divine Aura, that is what radiates from God Himself, the nearness to God, that is, the next world, the Paradises, that is why the Paradises have no suffering and no evil, because they are too near to the Absolute.

Q (indistinct):

A: Distance? Well, again, this has to be—it does create distance in this world, I mean, obviously, when this radiates—when a light radiates, it radiates till it finally dies out to nothing. I mean, when we have got to light something, then you can see that for yourself. The light radiates as far as it can, and then it becomes very faint in the distance, and you can say that that is symbolic or prophetic enough.

But then there are mysteries which one cannot understand, one might say, and in any case God is always acting to prevent evil to put things right, continually acting in this world; but "a thousand years in His sight are but as yesterday." It is not in His nature to be always interfering, but He does interfere a great deal. Religion after religion is brought to put things right; when anything goes wrong in the world it is put right, but it takes time...

Index

www.ingramcontent.com/pod-product-compliance
Lightning Source LLC
LaVergne TN
LVHW041156080426
835511LV00006B/619
9781908092090